ON THE
SHORES OF
PERGA

How John Mark's Departure from the First Pauline
Missionary Journey Changed the Gentile World

ERBEY GALVAN VALDEZ

FOREWORD BY DR. RUDOLPH GONZALEZ

WESTBOW
PRESS®
A DIVISION OF THOMAS NELSON
& ZONDERVAN

WestBow Press books may be ordered through booksellers or by contacting:

WestBow Press
A Division of Thomas Nelson & Zondervan
1663 Liberty Drive
Bloomington, IN 47403
www.westbowpress.com
1 (866) 928-1240

ISBN: 978-1-9736-9505-9 (sc)
ISBN: 978-1-9736-9507-3 (hc)
ISBN: 978-1-9736-9506-6 (e)

Library of Congress Control Number: 2020912314

Print information available on the last page.

WestBow Press rev. date: 07/08/2020

CONTENTS

FOREWORD

"All's well that ends well," or so goes the saying many people take as a sigh of great relief, especially when a critical outcome would seem to be in doubt, hanging in the balance as it were.

After reading *On the Shores of Perga,* I am convinced Erbey Valdez has advanced the needle in New Testament scholarship, strengthening the view of John Mark's actions as reflecting a theological/cultural crisis as big as any at the earliest beginnings of the Christian community. Of course, it's not that the issues, vehemently upheld by the Judaizers, aren't evident in Saint Paul's epistles, but these who are identified as the "circumcision party" are regularly depicted by the apostle as outsiders, bent on inserting their false gospel, requiring Gentile believers to uphold their Mosaic legalities. That said, to propose that John Mark may also have been a proponent of such views brings the problem closer to home than anyone may have realized heretofore.

To argue his perspective, Valdez puts forth a thoughtful theory for John Mark's departure from Paul's first missionary excursion, and it has nothing to do with an immature young man experiencing physical ailment, malaria, or perhaps homesickness. To be sure, Mark's departure from the team happens abruptly, and illness or homesickness provides a convenient, albeit stereotypical, foil for his actions, but is this definitive? As Valdez shows, the Christian canon does not leave the reader with adolescent immaturity as the only possible explanation. As his insightful study reveals, Erbey Valdez applies the tools of historical and grammatical study to Luke's usage of names to help us consider a more culturally attuned assessment, and one that resonates with the challenge that Judaizers posed throughout the tenure of Paul's service.

As the book of Acts reveals, the full implications of outreach to the

Gentile world could not be held up. Already, Gentiles were receiving the gospel with enthusiasm. And in response to the widening opportunity, the student of Gamaliel was all too eager to set aside his Hebrew name for a Gentile *nomen* palatable to Gentile sensibilities, but what of longstanding Jewish boundary issues? For Valdez, John Mark's actions were principled rather than opportunistic, and it is to his credit that he stuck to his view of the gospel rather than violate his conscience. But biblical Christianity is nothing if it doesn't confront the stated beliefs of people, and John Mark was surely challenged. Through his writings, Luke shows how Mark would yield and give way to the inexorable force of the gospel. In time, Mark came to understand that the good news of Jesus was for all people, Jew and Gentile alike, and it was based on faith and apart from the works of the law. Indeed, all's well that ends well!

Rudolph D. Gonzalez
March 12, 2020

PREFACE

In approximately AD 48, the apostle Paul, his coworker Barnabas, and Barnabas's cousin, John Mark, boarded a ship at Seleucia and headed for Cyprus to initiate what is now known as the first Pauline missionary journey. Set apart by the Holy Spirit and commissioned by the church at Antioch, these three men began a mission that, in retrospect, can be counted among the most pivotal events in world history. It is difficult to imagine that these men were cognizant of the impact their work would ultimately have upon the early Christian church, and especially in regard to Gentile Christianity. During this mission, an unexpected setback occurred—John Mark left Paul and Barnabas shortly after their arrival at Perga in Pamphylia and returned to Jerusalem. Although Luke offers no immediate details for Mark's departure, the events that would unfold point to an unprecedented movement that occurs within the Gentile mission. For most scholars, there is no question that Gentile evangelism posed a serious challenge to primitive Christianity, but the reason for Mark's departure from the first mission remains largely a mystery. Some regard Luke's mention of Mark's departure as but a mere side note to the story. For others, Mark's actions spark curiosity but remain clouded within the narrative. Is it possible that Luke intended for Mark's departure to serve as a critical juncture to the Gentile controversy that immediately unfolded?

John Mark, more commonly referred to as simply Mark, has always held a particular fascination for me.[1] Not many can claim the privilege of having worked alongside the two great pillars of the early church: Peter

---

[1] I will use the names Mark and John Mark interchangeably, but with the nuanced intention of using John Mark when referring to events prior to the Jerusalem Council, and Mark when referring to post-Jerusalem Council events. This reflects the Lukan pattern of Acts. See chapter 3 on discussion of Lukan name patterns.

and Paul. This is particularly significant because of the distinct ministries for which they were called. As Peter was called to the Jews, so Paul was called to the Gentiles (Gal. 2:7). In the midst of the work of these two giants of the Christian faith, there stood Mark. Luke, as presumed author of Acts,[2] presents Mark as a character who flows between the ministries of these two men. In various scenes, he is found praying for Peter's release in Jerusalem (Acts 12:12), ministering with Paul and Barnabas at Antioch (12:25), assisting on the first missionary journey to Asia Minor (13:5), watching intently from behind the scenes at the Jerusalem Council, sailing to Cyprus with Barnabas (15:39), reconnecting with Peter at Rome (1 Pet. 5:13), and serving Paul in his final days while in Rome (2 Tim. 4:11). In certain ways, Mark appears to function as a bridge between the Jewish and Gentile worlds, and perhaps for this reason, Luke placed Mark at the crux of the Jewish-Gentile controversy that occupies so much of his focus in Acts.

When I first began to examine this narrative, I was in the master of divinity program at Southwestern Baptist Theological Seminary. In my research, I was struck by Mark's departure in Acts 13:13 and wondered why Luke did not expound on this event. I was also confused by how few NT scholars had explored its possibilities or implications. Was Mark's departure from the first mission as insignificant as its brevity implied? Despite the apparently casual reference, I sensed something profound behind Mark's withdrawal. Yet, I also remembered Thomas Campbell's warning, "Where the Scriptures speak, we speak; and where the Scriptures are silent, we are silent."[3] I assumed it was because of Campbell's principle that so many scholars were reluctant to press too far on this episode, lest they commit the fallacy of presumption. However, as I continued to examine the events that soon followed, I became more and more convinced that the scriptures were not entirely silent on this issue. Indeed, Luke

---

[2] This text assumes Lukan authorship with an estimated date of circa AD 70 (see footnote 214). For more thorough discussion on authorship of Acts, see Craig S. Keener, *Acts: An Exegetical Commentary*, vol. 1 (Grand Rapids, MI: Baker Academic, 2012), 402–22.

[3] James Leo Garrett Jr., *Baptist Theology: A Four-Century Study* (Macon, GA: Mercer University Press, 2014), 252–53.

appeared to leave literary clues at every turn, all apparently connecting Mark to the emerging Gentile mission.

When I compared Mark's actions on the first mission with his entire life of ministry, I was struck by its oddity. It seemed to me as if Luke was saying that something significant had occurred to Mark during that first mission that had never occurred before … nor would it happen again. Mark's decision to return to Jerusalem, and not Antioch, also seemed unusual to the flow of Luke's plot. Amazingly, as suddenly as he departed the first mission, Mark was ready and willing to join Paul and Barnabas on their second mission! Thus, it also seemed as if Luke was saying that something significant had occurred to Mark in the events that soon followed. Was Luke contextualizing Mark within his narrative in order to depict the Jewish transformation toward the Gentile mission?

Over the course of my seminary studies, I continued to work on this theory until it eventually became the subject of my thesis for my master of theology degree at Liberty University. Now that I have begun my doctoral work at Columbia International University, I have returned to this present work in order to strengthen my research using the critical methods I have explored. I have restructured my original thesis into a narrative form and applied a literary-critical analysis in order to better illustrate certain Lukan clues within the text. I have also applied socio-historical methods to recover certain aspects of the *Sitz im Leben* (life-setting) of the church community for which Luke wrote his gospel. The Jewish-Gentile controversy seems to be at the forefront of this community, and it certainly appears most prevalent in Luke's writing.

We know that prior to Paul's first missiological venture, Gentiles had been admitted into the Jewish faith through a process known as "proselytization," the practice of Jewish conversion in which a Gentile submits to aspects of the Mosaic Law, including circumcision, dietary food restrictions, and observance of Jewish holidays. This practice naturally transitioned into the Christian movement since it began within the Jewish faith. It is also evident that the gospel message had been preached to Gentiles prior to Paul's first missionary incursion into Asia Minor (Acts 8:26–40, 11:20). What we do not see, at least not formally, is the intentional evangelism of the Gentiles apart from submission to elements of the Mosaic Law. Although Peter's witness to Cornelius and his household opened the gateway to the Gentile movement (10:34–48), Peter was never called as an apostle to the Gentiles, nor intentionally directed an evangelism toward the Gentiles after this historic event. However, what was initiated through Peter became a precedent for Paul. Luke's first reference to Gentile evangelism, free and clear of the requirements of proselytization, occurs only after Mark departs from the first mission. Immediately after Mark departs for Jerusalem, Paul and Barnabas begin their new evangelistic work to the Gentiles (13:46–48), and this may not be a coincidence.

This book will examine the viability of the idea that John Mark's departure was motivated by theological differences with Paul that the gospel message could be offered to the Gentiles without the traditional requirements of Jewish proselytization. A theological rift may have occurred between Mark and Paul between their departure from Paphos and their arrival at Perga in Pamphylia. Paul may have shared his newly inspired missionary objective with John Mark and Barnabas to evangelize to the Gentiles that salvation in Christ was possible without the requirement of submission to the Mosaic traditions. The success of Paul's new mission to the Gentiles is there for all to see, but the controversy that resulted soon after is equally apparent. The book of Acts describes the dissension that continued to build over the requirements of Gentile membership and the qualifications for Jewish-Gentile table fellowship within the Christian church, until it eventually climaxed at the Jerusalem Council. Luke may have intended for Mark's departure from the first missionary journey to serve as the distinct event that sparked the Gentile controversy into motion. Thus, John Mark's departure from the first Pauline missionary journey may have been theologically motivated, based on his view that the Gentiles could not live sanctified lives apart from submission to specific ceremonial Second-Temple idiosyncrasies.

Conceptually, this text will focus on the possibility of John Mark's departure as motivated by his theological differences with Paul on the issues of Gentile salvation in relation to the Mosaic Law. The question will be posed, what motivated this young missionary to abandon the first missionary journey, and what implications did his actions have upon the early church? I will argue that the theological differences between John Mark and Paul on soteriology offer the best explanation. I believe this view best explains both why Mark returned to Jerusalem and not Antioch (the church that commissioned their missionary journey). It also answers why the leaders from Judea seemed to know so much about Paul's activities while in Asia and how they were so readily present at Antioch upon their return. The Jerusalem Council was convened soon after, but despite the apparent resolution reached at Jerusalem, Barnabas and Mark were severed from Paul's immediate missionary work. There is no indication that Paul and Barnabas ever worked together again. So also, Mark would be divided from Paul for several years until they eventually reconciled. This analysis suggests that Luke did not intend for Mark's departure to serve as merely a parenthetical note to his account, but rather as the springboard to one of the greatest theological challenges facing the early church in the evangelization of the Gentiles. The Jerusalem Council's decision to accept the Gentiles without requirements of the Mosaic Law may have also served as the basis for Mark's decision to return with Paul and Barnabas on the second journey, and his eventual reconciliation with Paul (Col. 4:10–11, 2 Tim. 4:11).

The aim and purpose of this work is to present a fresh perspective on Mark's life and ministry by reexamining the events surrounding his departure at Perga in Pamphylia. Church history has perhaps misrepresented Mark in two ways. First, it may have underestimated Mark's role and function within the nascent Christian church, and primarily within the Jewish-Gentile movement. Second, Mark's departure from the first Pauline expedition may not have been grounded in a weak character or based upon a lack of fervor to complete the mission, as some scholars have suggested.[4] What if Mark was not a fickle, homesick, or weak missionary? What if he was a man of conviction, albeit misplaced in his allegiance to the Torah? What if Mark was reluctant to embrace the new faith-based Gentile movement because he stood fervently (and stubbornly) upon his Jewish identity as the mode and means of salvation? These are the questions that this text will explore.

A brief acknowledgment is in order before we begin our journey. I am indebted to so many people who have encouraged me throughout this work, and I am afraid I cannot list them all. I would first like to thank

---

[4] See the subchapter below, "John Mark "Departs" from the First Missionary Journey," in chapter 3, for a survey of the prevalent theories surrounding Mark's departure.

all my professors at Southwestern Baptist Theological Seminary, Liberty University, and Columbia International University. I have been equipped as both a minister and writer because of your devotion to your craft. I would like to specifically thank Dr. Rudy Gonzalez, my friend and mentor, and the person with whom I chose to first share my theory. Thank you for inspiring me to explore further. Your words of encouragement still resonate in my ears: "Erbey, I think you may be on to something here!" I am also indebted to Dr. Daniel Sheard, my professor and mentor at Liberty University, who provided critical academic analysis and input in the writing of my master's thesis. This product would never have come to fruition without your invaluable insight. I must also acknowledge Dr. Robert J. Dixon, my professor of Greek Syntax at Liberty University. You blessed me with a careful eye in examining my manuscript, as well as an encouraging word to work through the details in order to offer my best work for the Kingdom. I am also grateful to my doctoral professors at Columbia International University: Dr. David Croteau and Dr. John D. Harvey. Dr. Croteau, I am grateful for the opportunity to continue my academic journey and for your encouragement to keep my eyes focused on what is ahead. Dr. Harvey, thank you for challenging me to aim for progress and not perfection. I am also thankful to New Spirit Baptist Church, San Antonio, Texas, where I have had the privilege to serve as pastor and the opportunity to lecture on portions of my research. A pastor could not have a better flock. Finally, I give thanks for my wife, Maricruz. Without your support, I would not have been able to complete this project. Your love has sustained me all these years. You are the perfect pastor's wife and God's great gift to me in my ministry.

Erbey Valdez
June 2020

CHAPTER 1

AN IDENTITY CRISIS UNFOLDS

*T*he story of the first-generation Christian church began with an identity crisis. Although the book of Acts describes the NT church as enduring numerous attacks of persecution, heretical teachings, and false prophets, it appears that the challenge of transitioning the gospel message from the Jewish world to the Gentiles brought on an unanticipated crisis of identity. As Jewish believers began to embrace Jesus as the Messiah, they quickly discovered that Jesus could not simply become an addendum to their Jewish faith. Somehow, they were now different in their identity in comparison to their unbelieving Jewish brethren. For generations, the Jews had prided themselves as the "apple of God's eye" (Ps. 17:8), the elected sons of God, and holy and treasured possessions set apart from the world (Deut. 14:2). Now a new day had come through the resurrection of Christ. The people of Israel, once set apart as holy, were now commissioned to engage the world they had eluded for so long and share the message of Christ resurrected. The Gentile, once despised and held at arm's length, would now be invited to share in the righteousness of Christ and join the Christian community. For many Jews, the inclusion of Gentiles in the new kingdom ushered in by Christ was one thing, but to embrace a new spirit of identity that placed the Gentiles at the seat of the same communion table was totally unanticipated. F. F. Bruce notes that "the cleavage between Jew and Gentile was for Judaism the most radical within the human race."[5]

---

[5] F. F. Bruce, *The Epistle to the Galatians*, New International Greek Testament

Could the chasm that had existed for so long between Jew and Gentile be finally overcome?

Until the beginning of the Christian church, Gentiles were admitted into the Jewish community only as "proselytes," converts to the faith through ritual *mikvah* washings,[6] and submission to aspects of the Torah, such as dietary restrictions, observance of holy days, and circumcision. Any Gentile unwilling to submit fully to these prerequisites would find only limited access and acceptance by the Jewish community. Thus, when the new Christian movement began with the Gentile community, it began with the traditional prerequisites of Torah observance in mind. However, God never intended to save the world through the Mosaic covenant but by the Abrahamic covenant. God's covenant with Abraham promised that all the families of the earth would be blessed through Abraham's seed (Gen. 12:3). That promised seed had now been fulfilled in Jesus Christ who, by His death and resurrection, had brought salvation to the world beyond the Jews (Gal. 3:16).

If Gentiles had already been allowed within Judaism, then why would this issue now stir up so much controversy? Two answers stand at the fore. First, Paul challenged the traditional belief of Torah observance as the standard marker of the covenant relationship with God. He insisted that the new indicator was now evidenced by faith in Christ (Gal. 3:28–29). However, some Jewish Christians likely felt that "identity within the Mosaic covenant should take precedence over identity in Christ"[7] and thus viewed any member who did not honor this tradition as less than equal. Second, until the first Pauline mission, Gentile proselytes had consisted of only a small minority in Judaism. Perhaps up to this point

---

Commentary, I. Howard Marshall, and W. Ward Gasque, ed. (Grand Rapids, MI: William B. Eerdmans, 1982), 188.

[6] Mikvahs were baths used in Orthodox Judaism for the purpose of ritual purification, including as a purification rite for proselytes. The numerous *mikva'ot* excavated around Jerusalem by archaeologists, with most dating from the midsecond century BC to the first century AD, reveal their importance to Second Temple Judaism. For more information, see "mikvah," *The Lexham Bible Dictionary*, J. D. Barry, D. Bomar, D. R. Brown, R. Klippenstein, D. Mangum, C. Sinclair Wolcott, W. Widder, eds. (Bellingham, WA: Lexham Press, 2016).

[7] Jerry L. Sumney, *Paul: Apostle and Fellow Traveler* (Nashville, TN: Abingdon Press, 2014), 42.

the church leaders did not see a need for a unified theological position concerning Gentiles. Yet circumstances changed quickly when Gentiles became more prominent, especially at Antioch, where its members were predominantly, but not exclusively, Gentile.[8] Suddenly, the Christian church encountered the great question of determining how to define the people of God. The Christian church now faced an identity crisis. Even more challenging was the fact that there already existed a wide diversity of people within the Christian church, both Jew and Gentile, each with their own understanding of personal identity.

If the Abrahamic covenant had demonstrated a plan of salvation beyond the Jews and indeed for the whole world, then why did the inclusion of Gentiles become such a divisive issue in the early church? The answer is found in the basis of identity for the Jews. To be a Jew was to be a child of Abraham (John 8:39). To be a child of Abraham was to be elected by God. To be the elect of God meant that one lived a life set apart as holy from the world (Deut. 14:2). To live a life set apart as holy was only by means of the Torah (Josh. 1:8). For the Jew, the Torah was the means of the covenant, and circumcision was its symbol. Esteemed British NT scholar James Dunn rightly notes that the covenant that identified Israel as a people and the seed of Abraham was circumcision. "No circumcision, no covenant, no promise, no nation."[9] Thus, when the Christian movement began, many Jews remained steadfast in their belief that Gentiles could only don the identity of Christ by means of the Torah. Otherwise, how could the Gentile be made eligible for table fellowship? Before Christ leveled the playing field, the Torah had served as the modus operandi for the Jews, and to ask them to set it aside for the new cause of Christ was, in some sense, a call to surrender their own identity.

This new identity in Christ seemed to be the focus of Paul's writings. Paul did not refute that the children of Abraham were those who lived under the covenant promise of God, but he argued that the true children of Abraham were now identified by faith in Christ and not a presumed racial identity (Rom. 9:7–8). Nor did Paul argue for the abolition of Jewish identity or even the Torah itself. Rather, Paul insisted in the retainment

---

[8] Ibid.

[9] James D. G. Dunn, *Beginning from Jerusalem,* Christianity in the Making, vol. 2 (Grand Rapids, MI: William B. Eerdmans, 2009), 439.

of a Jew's own cultural identity but argued that one's cultural identity could never serve as the basis for spiritual salvation (Phil. 3:3–11). Thus, for Paul, it was pointless to place such requisites upon the Gentiles. Paul never argued that one's "Jewishness" was no longer relevant, nor did he ever cast away his own identity as a Jew. Krister Stendahl, an NT scholar and professor at Harvard University, stressed this point by arguing that Paul's encounter with Christ on the Damascus Road was more a "call" than a "conversion."

> It thus becomes clear that the usual conversion model of Paul the Jew who gives up his former faith to become a Christian is not the model of Paul but of ours. Rather, his call brings him to a new understanding of his mission, a new understanding of the law which is otherwise an obstacle to the Gentiles. His ministry is based on the specific conviction that the Gentiles will become a part of the people of God without having to pass through the law. This is Paul's secret revelation and knowledge.[10]

Simply put, Paul had discovered a new identity in Christ, and this new identity could not be attained by means of the Mosaic law, for the promise given to Abraham by God came before the Mosaic law (Gal. 3:17). Additionally, because Abraham had received God's covenantal promise long before Moses and the Mosaic law, Abraham himself was a converted Gentile! With the preaching of the kerygma to the Gentiles without the requirements of Torah traditions, a new message with a new purpose emerged, but not all Jewish Christians were ready to embrace the new Gentile cause.

By setting aside the Torah as a requisite for Gentile admission into the Christian community, Jews were now being challenged to reconsider the basis of their own identity. This newfound theology was a serious challenge to traditional Jews, who commonly viewed themselves as the "light for the nations" (Isa. 49:6) and the Gentiles as an inferior, and perhaps even

---

[10] Krister Stendahl, *Paul among Jews and Gentiles* (Philadelphia: Fortress Press, 1978), 9.

unsalvageable, people. Dr. Rudy Gonzalez,[11] a leading scholar both in NT and cultural philosophy, makes the critical observation that all cultures have redeemable value. He notes that "God always looks for something of redeemable value, but it must be on his terms."[12] Yet what we find at this juncture in salvation history is the Jews attempting to redeem the Gentiles on their terms and not God's. As the Gentile was called out of darkness to embrace a new faith in Christ, so the Jew was called to set aside his or her identity through the Mosaic Law and embrace a new life of faith in Christ. Imagine the turmoil that many traditional Jews faced at the thought of embracing a new foundation of faith, a new basis of spiritual identity— one that made Jew and Gentile equals in the eyes of God! How would the Jewish culture identify itself within the new Christian movement? More importantly, what identity did God intend to bestow upon the infant Christian church?

Paul: A Champion for the Gentiles

When the church began to take evangelism beyond Judea and to it surrounding regions, Paul stood front and center. Although evangelization to the Gentiles, per se, was not foreign to the Jewish agenda, the invitation to receive the gospel and join the Christian community apart from the adoption of elements of the Mosaic Law rocked many Jewish Christians to their core. In this great trial, no one was more equipped for the challenge than Paul. Paul not only lived and taught amid his sociocultural settings, his ministry and theology were very likely directly affected by them. Paul was raised in a "rich educational milieu" at Tarsus, a city steeped in Stoicism that served as an "important educational center in the ancient world."[13]

---

[11] Rudy Gonzalez currently serves as adjunct chair of biblical and theological studies at Baptist University of the Americas in San Antonio, Texas. Among his many distinctions, Dr. Gonzalez served as vice president of Southwestern Baptist Theological Seminary, director of Interfaith Evangelism for North American Mission Board, and the translation team of the Modern English Bible version in 2014.

[12] Rudolph D. Gonzalez, *Then Came Hispangelicals: The Rise of the Hispanic Evangelical and Why It Matters* (Sisters, OR: Deep River Books, 2019), 153.

[13] John McRay, *Paul: His Life and Teaching* (Grand Rapids, MI: Baker Academic, 2004), 23.

Thomas Schreiner[14] notes that "Paul made a lasting impact precisely because he tackled the specific circumstances in the churches from a worldview that was powerfully coherent."[15] Perhaps it was this background and influence that Paul spoke of when he said that the mystery of the gospel that God revealed to him was in the "stewardship" (οἰκονομία) given to him for the Gentiles (Eph. 3:2). In other words, Paul felt both equipped and personally responsible for delivering the message of salvation to the Gentiles.

Although Paul's background must be acknowledged as part of God's plan of redemption for the Gentiles, ultimately Paul's revelation of Jesus Christ shifted his theology. As Martin Luther discovered that a reform was needed in the theology of the Roman church at the onset of the Reformation, so Paul recognized a need for theological reform in his own Jewish faith. The theology he had clung to all his life now clashed with the revelation he had received from Christ. No one captured the oppositional texture of Paul's newfound theology with the Rabbinic Judaism of his time more than Martin Hengel, one of the great twentieth century German theologians of the Tübingen School and expert in Second Temple history. Hengel demonstrated that Paul's encounter with the risen Christ led him to recognize that "the way to salvation indicated by the Torah and God's crucified Messiah *must inevitably stand in fundamental opposition*."[16] The two were as oil and water, and no concessions could be made.

After his conversion, and prior to the events leading up to the first commission to Asia, Paul had met with the disciples in Jerusalem in order to determine his place in the church but was unsuccessful because they were afraid of him (Acts 9:26). As a result, Paul was ostracized from the church at Jerusalem, arguably the center of the early Christian movement, for the first few years following his conversion to Christianity. Chronologically, it seems most likely that a span of several years transpired between his ministering in Damascus and his return to Jerusalem (9:23). A delay in

---

[14] Thomas R. Schreiner is James Buchanan Harrison Professor of NT Interpretation and associate dean at the Southern Baptist Theological Seminary in Louisville, KY. Mr. Schreiner is not only a leading NT scholar, but also one of today's foremost authorities in Pauline studies.

[15] Thomas R. Schreiner, *Paul: Apostle of God's Glory in Christ* (Downers Grove, IL: InterVarsity Press, 2001), 39.

[16] Emphasis added. Martin Hengel, *Acts and the History of Earliest Christianity*, John Bowden, trans. (Eugene, OR: Wipf and Stock, 2003), 83–84.

Paul's return to Jerusalem by several years also best explains the skepticism he received at the hands of the Jerusalem church, who would have likely reasoned that if Paul had a real conversion, it would have resulted in an immediate return.[17] That skepticism may have been heightened when Paul began to petition for the Gentiles. From the perspective of some of the conservative Jews in Jerusalem, Paul may have been viewed as operating beyond the authority of the church with his new agenda for the Gentiles. Did this background frame the initial tension between Paul's mission and the Jerusalem church that would later erupt after Mark's departure? As the years passed for Paul with no word of inclusion or support from the Jerusalem leaders, "it is not difficult to imagine Paul feeling that he had been marginalized by his Jewish brothers in Judea, who did not yet understand that it was time for the Gentiles to be enthusiastically evangelized, and that they were to be accepted without conversion to Judaism as a prerequisite (15:1)."[18]

Understanding Paul's richly diverse cultural background may also help in understanding Mark's departure from his first missiological venture. If Mark was indeed theologically motivated to leave the mission because his ideology clashed with Paul's new mission to the Gentiles, then Paul's early exposure to Greco-Roman culture in Cilicia, as opposed to Mark's more rigid Hebrew background in Jerusalem, may have played a significant role in the matter. Mark was likely discipled by Peter in Jerusalem, an instruction that would have been more conservative and traditional in its approach to Jewish Christian practice, in comparison to Paul's. The former Pharisee, on the other hand, was trained by Gamaliel, a rabbi who subscribed to the Hillel view, which took "a more commonsense approach to matters"[19] than the more conservative Shammai school of thought. Thus, Paul was more able to adapt to the inclusion of the Gentiles in the new faith by making "the necessary adjustments to embrace the new circumstances."[20] This zealous man from Tarsus, more than anyone,

---

[17] Darrell L. Bock, *Acts*, Baker Exegetical Commentary on the New Testament, Robert W. Yarbrough and Robert H. Stein, ed. (Grand Rapids, MI: Baker Academic, 2007), 369.

[18] McRay, 98.

[19] Ibid., 45.

[20] Ibid.

understood this diversity that existed behind both the Jewish and Gentile identity. Rudolf Bultmann[21] understood how critical Paul's background was to both his success with the Gentiles and Hellenistic Christianity: "The historical presupposition for Paul's theology is not the kerygma of the oldest Church but that of the Hellenistic Church."[22] Thus, when the Gentile challenge was posed, Paul emerged as its champion. Although his methods aligned more with Jewish Hellenism, they were also more at odds with traditional Jews, such as John Mark.

Greeks, Proselytes, and "God-Fearers"

The cultural identity of the NT church cannot be divided as simply as Jew and Gentile. Rather, different classes existed among both groups, and it seems that when it came to Christian table fellowship, the divisive barriers became even more apparent. Although the sociocultural atmosphere in first-century Palestine was much more complicated than the simpler outline offered here, the major distinctions between Jews and Gentiles seemed to occupy the focus of Luke's narrative, and particularly in regard to the Gentile controversy. The sociocultural divisions were primarily divided over the role of the Torah (Mosaic Law) in the life of the individual, and this became a central concern regarding how the Torah should apply to the Gentiles. Although the Torah appears as the consistent measure of the covenant community, it also appears that the literature of Second Temple Judaism "contributed different, and sometimes contradictory, pictures of what defined God's people,"[23] especially in regard to Gentiles. For example, traditional Rabbinic Jews, such as the Pharisees, insisted that Gentiles were "under obligation to keep the whole Jewish Law," while Hellenistic Judaism held to the belief that circumcision and the keeping of the cultic commandments was not as crucial as belief in one God and following

---

[21] Rudolf Karl Bultmann (1884–1976) was a German Lutheran theologian and professor of the NT at the University of Marburg. He is widely recognized as one of the major figures of early-20th-century NT biblical studies.

[22] Rudolf Bultmann, *Theology of the New Testament*, translated by Kendrick Grobel (Waco, TX: Baylor University Press, 2007), 63.

[23] A. Chadwick Thornhill, *The Chosen People: Election, Paul and Second Temple Judaism* (Downers Grove, IL: InterVarsity Press, 2015), 99.

"the basic ethical demands of the OT."[24] Hence, this theological variance between the "Hebrews" and Hellenists may have been the source of their division in the Gentile controversy outlined in Acts, and the cause for the dispute that arose in Acts 6:1.

The different references and descriptions of the Gentiles in the NT were largely dependent upon their status within the Jewish community. From the perspective of the Jews, the Gentiles could be classified in three general ways:

1. "Greeks" (Ἕλλην), referred to all non-Jews without any particular indication of religious identity.[25] Although, the term "always means a Greek of Gentile origin,"[26] it was often used to describe the pagan Gentiles in general. Although most Jews avoided the "Greeks" regarding table fellowship, this group served as the focus of Gentile evangelism in the early Christian church. In Galatians 3:28, Paul declares that there is "neither Jew nor Greek," and uses the term Ἕλλην to refer to Greeks in general. Paul likely used the three couplets in this section (Greeks, slaves, and women) in order to counter against the three *bĕrākôt*, or benedictions, that Jews recited in their morning prayers, "Blessed by He [God] that He did not make me a Gentile; blessed be He that He did not make me a boor [slave]; blessed be He that He did not make me a woman."[27] Such benedictions reveal the deep-rooted prejudice that Jews held against the Gentiles.

2. "Proselytes" (προσήλυτος), were Gentiles who converted to Judaism through full submission of the Torah, including circumcision (Acts 2:11). The Gentile "proselyte" was a term

---

[24] Karl G. Kuhn, "προσήλυτος" in *Theological Dictionary of the New Testament*, vol. VI. Gerhard Friedrich, ed. Geoffrey W. Bromiley, trans. and ed. (Grand Rapids, MI: William B. Eerdmans, 1968), 739.

[25] The term "Greeks" (Ἕλλην), should not be confused with the term Ἑλληνιστής, which refers to a Greek-speaking Jew and is referred to as "Hellenists" in Scripture (Acts 6:1). For more information, see F. F. Bruce, *The Epistle to the Galatians*, NIGTC (Grand Rapids, MI: William B. Eerdmans, 1982), 111.

[26] Richard N. Longenecker, *Galatians,* Word Biblical Commentary, vol. 41, Ralph P. Martin, ed. (Dallas, TX: Word Books, 1990), 157.

[27] Ibid.

used to denote the Gentile who surrendered completely to the Jewish faith by completing a three-part rite of circumcision, the mikvah ceremonial washing, and the offering of a sacrifice in the temple.[28] William Barclay notes that after completing the first two requirements, the man would undergo a "Jewish baptism," where he would make a confession of faith before three men, called "fathers of baptism," who would read portions of the law to him and pronounce blessings.[29] When the new proselyte emerged, he would become a member of the Jewish faith, in accordance with the Levitical rites of purification (Lev. 11–15). Sadly, despite the opportunity for Gentiles to cross the gulf that existed between Jews and Gentiles through proselytization, the gulf often remained.[30]

3. "Godfearers" (θεοσεβής or φοβούμενος τὸν Θεόν), were Gentiles who had adopted Judaism but without full submission to Torah, especially circumcision (Acts 10:2). Compared to the Gentile proselytes, the Gentile "Godfearers" attended synagogue worship, believed in Jewish monotheism, and observed some aspects of the ceremonial law, but did not submit to full conversion by circumcision.[31] For many Gentiles, the act of circumcision was seen as a form of bodily mutilation and an abomination in the Greek world. For this reason, circumcision became a major barrier for early Christian evangelism to the Gentiles. Therefore, Paul warned the Gentiles to "look out for those who mutilate the flesh" (Phil. 3:1–11), masterfully using the Judaizers' own argument for circumcision against them. However, the limited submission to Torah does not imply that Gentile "Godfearers" lived completely Law-free, since they were expected to at least adhere to the seven universal laws that comprised the Noachic Law (Gen. 9:1–17).[32] However, in the eyes of many traditional Jews, the observance of

---

[28] Kuhn, 738.

[29] William Barclay, *The Letters to the Galatians and Ephesians*, The New Daily Study Bible (Louisville, KY: Westminister John Knox Press, 2002), 38.

[30] Bruce, *The Epistle to the Galatians*, 188.

[31] Kuhn, 731.

[32] Michelle Slee, *The Church in Antioch in the First Century C.E.: Communion and Conflict*, Sheffield Journal for the Study of the New Testament Supplement Series. Stanley E. Porter, ed. (New York: T & T Clark International, 2003), 21.

the Noachic Law without circumcision and relative observance of the Law meant that "Godfearers" remained second-class citizens and were still treated as Gentiles in table fellowship.

A clear indicator of the difference in the way Gentile proselytes and "Godfearers" were treated by the Jewish community is through recent archaeological discoveries of Jewish burial practices in first century Palestine. Although proselytes were allowed to be buried in the Jewish cemeteries, both in Jerusalem and throughout the Diaspora, "Godfearers" were not.[33] Needless to say, in the eyes of the Jewish community, Gentile proselytes demonstrated a much deeper commitment to their conversion by submitting to circumcision, than their Gentile "Godfearer" brothers. Although both Gentile groups were willing to observe the kosher diet during Jewish fellowship meals, many Christian Jews believed circumcision determined their eligibility in sharing the Lord's Supper. This practice of exclusion from table fellowship carried over into the Christian community and became a powder keg for the first-generation Christian church.

"Hebrews" and Hellenists

The question of the Torah in the application of the Christian community affected Jew and Gentile alike, for "there were different opinions regarding the role the Torah had to play in the lives of those who believed in Jesus, and these opinions were held by *both* Jewish and Gentile believers."[34] Thus, what we appear to find in our sociocultural analysis of first-century Palestine are clear splinters that existed, not only among Gentiles, but within the Jewish Christian community as well. The biblical text not only differentiates between the Orthodox Jews who rejected Jesus and the Christian Jews. One also finds Aramaic-speaking Jews, regarded as "Hebrews" (Ἑβραῖος),[35] and Greek-speaking Jews

---

[33] Hengel, 89.

[34] Slee, 10.

[35] Although the term "Hebrew" is commonly used to identify the ethnic name of the Israelites, those of the Pauline camp (including Luke) expanded the term to identify those Hebrew-Aramaic-speaking Israelites in contrast to a Greek-speaking Israelite. See W. Bauer, F. W. Danker, W. F. Arndt, and F. W. Gingrich, *A Greek-English*

known as "Hellenists" (Ἑλληνιστής), who were apparently divided over much more than language (Acts 6:1). As traditional Jews and Christian Jews were divided over the question of the Messiahship of Jesus, the "Hebrews" and Hellenists were Jewish Christians who were divided over the function of the Torah, especially regarding how it applied to Gentile table fellowship. Simply put, these two Jewish Christian groups regarded and interacted with the Gentiles in radically different ways. Hence, one might acknowledge three separate groups of Gentiles in the eyes of the Christian Jews: (1) Gentile nonbelievers, a group almost all Jews avoided; (2) Gentile proselytes, a group that most Hebrews and Hellenists accepted in table fellowship; and (3) "Godfearers," a group that the "Hebrews" generally rejected, but that most Hellenists permitted in table fellowship.

The "Hebrews" retained and spoke their native tongue of Aramaic and tended to apply the principles of Torah more strictly. As a result, they refused fellowship with Gentiles who had not submitted to proselytization ("Greeks" and even "Godfearers"). Some of the "Hebrews" went as far as refusing fellowship with all Gentiles, including proselytes, insisting that the hand of table fellowship be restricted to Jews alone. After Peter received his vision at Joppa and experienced the pouring out of the Holy Spirit upon the Gentiles at Caesarea, this more conservative group at Jerusalem, identified as the "circumcision party," criticized Peter for practicing table fellowship with uncircumcised Gentiles (Acts 11:2). Also, this same group stirred up controversy at Antioch, resulting in a direct confrontation between Peter and Paul (Gal. 2:11–14). Later, this group stood in protest against allowing Gentiles to enter the church apart from circumcision (Acts 15:5).

The Hellenists were Greek-speaking Jews and tended to apply the principles of the Torah more moderately. Because the Hellenists usually extended table fellowship to both Gentile proselytes and "Godfearers," their openness to the Gentiles resulted in a three-way division with the "Hebrews." First, they were divided by language, much in the same way that a modern church may be divided by different services offering different languages. Although many people in first-century Palestine likely spoke more than one language, a preferred and primary language would still exist. The church at Jerusalem possibly practiced two separate Christian

---

Lexicon of the New Testament and Other Early Christian Literature, 3rd ed. (Chicago: University of Chicago Press, 2000), 270.

services divided by language: one in Aramaic and the other in Greek (Acts 6:1). If so, then the separate services would have further isolated the "Hebrews" from both the Hellenists, who observed in Greek, and the Gentiles, who would have likely not spoken Aramaic and/or attended their services. If separate services were not practiced, there would at least have been separate table fellowship between the "Hebrews" and Hellenists (6:1). Second, because the primary language for Hellenists was Greek, their shared tongue with the Gentiles made for more open dialogue and fellowship. As a result, the climate of openness between the Hellenists and Gentiles, particularly in table fellowship, would have likely pushed the "Hebrews" further into isolation. Third, and perhaps most important, because the Hellenists tended to be more moderate in their application of the Torah in comparison to their "Hebrew" brethren, a theological schism emerged over the inclusion of the Gentiles in the Christian church. As the former argued that a new covenant had now emerged in Christ that no longer required placing the "yoke" of Torah submission upon the Gentiles (15:10), the latter insisted upon circumcision as the only means by which Gentiles could be redeemed (15:1).

Of the two divisions of Jewish Christians, John Mark would have most likely identified with the "Hebrews" of the "circumcision group" (Col. 4:11). When Luke first introduces Mark, he is praying for Peter's release from prison and apparently being discipled under Peter's wing (Acts 12:12). Although Peter is never directly regarded as a member of this "circumcision group" by Luke, the fact that he needs to explain his actions surrounding Gentile fellowship at Caesarea (Acts 11), and his catering to their table practices at Antioch (Gal. 2:12), suggests at least a prior allegiance. Thus, Mark's discipleship under Peter serves as a primary clue to the connection that Mark would have with the more traditional "Hebrews." Since Peter served as an ambassador to the Jews who had avoided fellowship with the Gentiles until his encounter with Cornelius (Acts 10:28), Mark would likely have been equally hesitant in embracing Gentile table fellowship. Mark remained closely aligned with Peter throughout his ministry (1 Pet. 5:13), and it can be viably argued that Mark's apparent change of heart and decision to return with Paul and Barnabas after the Council of Jerusalem was based, in no small measure, upon his mentor's endorsement of the new Gentile mission (Acts 15:7–11). All told, the diversity of soteriological views within the early Jewish-Christian community were based, in no small part, upon the complexities of election and identity. To this subject we now turn.

Election and Identity within Second Temple Judaism

One cannot truly appreciate the different factions present within the Jewish-Gentile controversy without first understanding what Jews, at the time, believed about election and identity as God's chosen people.[36] When Paul petitioned for the inclusion of Gentiles in the emerging Christian church, apart from the requirements of the Mosaic Law, something greater than racial prejudice or theological preference was at stake (although these issues were certainly present!) Rather, the identity as God's people by adherence to the covenantal law appeared to dominate the landscape of Jewish thought in Paul's day. It would thus appear that the culture surrounding the Jewish-Gentile controversy was much more volatile than simply a division based upon theological principles or cultural biases. Instead, for Jews of the "circumcision party" (Acts 11:2, 15:5; Phil. 3:2), the issue may have been fundamental to the question of election and what it meant to be identified as God's people.

The prevailing Jewish literature at the time appears to reflect a predominant Jewish perspective that defined the elect of God on both conditional and unconditional elements.[37] The striking point here is that election in Second Temple Judaism reflects less a "works-based" righteousness and more a righteousness that depends on both God's grace and the necessity of keeping the covenant promises by adhering to the Law.[38] As such, both election and identity appear to have been clearly defined by the Mosaic covenant (i.e., obedience to the Mosaic Law). From this perspective, Paul's new agenda to the Gentiles, as no longer entailing

---

[36] For a more thorough discussion on this topic, see A. Chadwick Thornhill's excellent analysis in *The Chosen People: Election, Paul and Second Temple Judaism* (Downers Grove, IL: IVP Academic, 2015).

[37] Thornhill, 41.

[38] Although numerous works have progressed this discussion, E. P. Sanders spearheaded this view away from the traditional belief of Judaism as a works-based faith through his concept of "covenantal nomism" in *Paul and Palestinian Judaism* (Philadelphia: Fortress Press, 1977).

submission to the Law, would have shocked many traditional Jews who believed that both individual and corporate election were primarily identified by the covenantal law. In other words, Paul's new mission would have undoubtedly threatened not only the traditional methods of Gentile proselytization, but also the Jewish notion of election and what it meant to be a member of God's covenant community, both nationally and individually. Indeed, Second Temple Judaism appears to have encompassed both national election and individual identity, based upon faithfulness to the Mosaic covenant. Simply put, Second Temple Judaism tended to view national election as something based upon the unconditional grace of God, while individual election was based upon the conditional obedience to the covenant law. E. P. Sanders, one of the leading proponents of the "New Perspective on Paul," argues that "Physical descent is the basis of the election, and the election is the basis of salvation, but physical descent from Jacob is not the sole condition of salvation."[39] Thus, for many Jews, the Gentile invitation to join the church apart from adherence to certain elements of Judaism was offensive, because the invitation was absent of the individual elements of the covenant.

Contrary to the popular assumption that Second Temple Judaism viewed Gentiles as excluded from the covenant community and all ethnic Jews as automatically included, the Jewish literature appears to paint a different picture. In actuality, the Gentile community was regularly accepted into the Jewish community as proselytes, with varying degrees of acceptance dependent upon their levels of submission to Torah (i.e., circumcision, dietary laws, etc.). In the Dead Sea Scrolls, the rules for membership in the covenant community (Community Rule), stated that atonement could only be found by the covenant, and that even outsiders (Gentiles) could enter into the covenant if they submitted to obeying its ordinances (1QS 3.7–12). For many Jews, membership in the covenant community could also mean the exclusion of ethnic Jews, since election was conditionally dependent upon submission and obedience to the covenantal law. Thus, leading up to the Gentile controversy that emerged at Antioch, Gentile admission to the covenantal community seems consistently based on adherence to the Torah. From this perspective,

---

[39] E. P. Sanders, *Paul and Palestinian Judaism* (Philadelphia: Fortress Press, 1977), 368.

John Mark may have viewed Paul's new Gentile agenda as an unacceptable breach of Judaism. Indeed, for Mark, admitting Gentiles as full members of God's community without the requirements of proselytization may have "smacked of abandoning the law as the guide for how God's people should live to be faithful to the covenant."[40]

For the reformed man of Tarsus, election and identity were available for both Jews and Gentiles, but the identifying marker had now shifted from the Mosaic Law to faith in Christ (1 Cor. 15:20–24, 2 Cor. 5:14–21). Paul did not invent these concepts of corporate election and identity since they already existed in Judaism, but the significance of the work of Christ completely "recalibrated" them.[41] In Romans 4:9–12, Paul not only declares Abraham's election and righteousness as separate from the Torah, but as "the father of all who believe without being circumcised" (v. 11), inverting the traditional Jewish view of Abraham, making him "the first Gentile convert whom God declared "right" apart from keeping the law."[42] Consequently, Paul's point on election and identity was plain— the fulfillment of God's plan for the elect could only come from outside of the law, not within it, since the law was intended to separate Jews and Gentiles. However, in Christ, God is one (Gal. 3:20). Paul was not necessarily attacking Jewish legalism, per se, but rather the attitude of Jewish exclusivism that rejected the idea that all were now justified by faith in Christ.[43] Stendahl contends that Paul's argument concerning the Jewish-Gentile situation was not secondary to his concept of justification by faith. Rather, "Paul was chiefly concerned about the relation between Jews and Gentiles—and in the development of *this* concern he used as one of his arguments the idea of justification by faith."[44]

For many ethnic Jews, this teaching would seriously challenge the standard for Jewish election and identity and the factors that determine membership in the covenantal community. For example, the law of

---

[40] Sumney, 99.

[41] Thornhill, 58.

[42] Ibid., 176.

[43] Jason C. Meyer, *The End of the Law: Mosaic Covenant in Pauline Theology*, NAC Studies in Bible & Theology, E. Ray Clendenen, ed. (Nashville, TN: B&H Academic, 2009), 6.

[44] Stendahl, 3.

circumcision was not merely an ethnic symbol of identity but, according to *Jubilees*, a "prerequisite for covenant membership" that would render both Gentiles and compromising Jews who rejected it as violators of the covenant destined for destruction (Jub. 15:25–34). Paul countered by arguing that Gentiles are marked spiritually, "not by the outward symbol of circumcision but rather by the greater sign of the Spirit."[45] This was no easy task for Paul, for to ask his Jewish opponents to allow Gentiles to enter into the covenant community apart from circumcision was not only a challenge to their views on Gentile membership, but also a direct challenge to their own identities as covenant members! However, the point was not that God was abandoning the Jewish people but rather that God was "redefining the nature of his people."[46] Was this redefinition the primary concern of the circumcision party leading up to the Council of Jerusalem? Did these questions ring in John Mark's ears when he first heard of Paul's new mission to the Gentiles on the way to Pamphylia? If so, then the warning bells would have been rung first within the axis of Gentile Christianity at the time—the church at Antioch.

---

[45] Craig S. Keener, *Galatians: A Commentary* (Grand Rapids, MI: Baker Academic, 2019), 259.

[46] Steve Walton, "Acts," *Theological Interpretation of the New Testament*, Kevin J. Vanhoozer, ed. (Grand Rapids, MI: Baker Academic, 2009), 76.

CHAPTER 2

THE GENTILE MOVEMENT
BEGINS TO RUMBLE

*W*hen the disciples of Jesus first began to preach Christ crucified, they did so to their own Jewish brethren in their houses of worship. The Messiahship of Christ was the central question, and the major division was found in either the Jews who believed in Christ resurrected, and those who did not. Thus, one can identify three features present in the early church movement: (1) the synagogue as the site of evangelism, (2) the Jews as the original recipients of the kerygma, and (3) Jesus of Nazareth as the central question of salvation. Later, when the Jewish Christian church began to take shape, a new element entered onto the scene—the Gentiles. Suddenly, the elemental image of the body of believers began to morph, and a new set of features emerged: (1) the Christians going beyond the synagogue to preach the gospel to the world, (2) the Gentiles as now included as recipients of the kerygma, and (3) although Jesus remained the central question in regard to salvation, the question of what other requirements must be asked of the Gentiles became a reality for the church.

As mentioned earlier, the disagreement first occurred between the "Hebrews" and Hellenists, who argued over whether the Torah should apply to the Gentile Christians in the same way that it had applied to Judaism. Nor was the Gentile issue limited to the Christian church, for even nonbelieving Jews would have been offended at the thought that the Hellenists were observing table fellowship with uncircumcised Gentiles. For conservative Jews, both Christian and non-Christian alike, it was an offense against Judaism to "take the children's bread and throw it to the dogs" (*Did.* 9:5, Matt. 15:26). This "common Jewish epithet,"[47] uttered by Jesus to the Canaanite woman, reflected the sense of Jewish national prejudice that Gentiles, like dogs, were unclean and unworthy creatures. Thus, one is left to wonder whether it was more offensive for the non-Christian Jews that some of their Jewish brethren were preaching Jesus as the Messiah or that some of their Jewish brethren were practicing table fellowship with Gentiles in direct violation of their Torah. Perhaps a better way to pose the question is, if the Jewish-Christian practice of table fellowship with uncircumcised Gentiles was offensive to other Jewish-Christians, how much more so to non-Christian Jews?

It does not seem a coincidence that, when the persecution broke out against the Christian church, it appeared specifically aimed at the Hellenistic Christian Jews (Acts 8:1). It also seems no coincidence that the Christians who remained in Jerusalem were of a largely "Hebrew" identity. Luke notes that the persecution resulted in the scattering throughout the regions of Judea and Samaria, "except the apostles" (8:1). This remnant group of conservative Jews would apparently press on in Jerusalem, largely void of the Jewish Hellenistic influence. What we find occurring in the Jerusalem church following the persecutions and leading up to the Jerusalem Council is a bend toward Jewish conservatism. The church of Jerusalem was where the "circumcision group" emerged (11:2). It was also from Jerusalem where the opposition to Paul's new agenda to the Gentiles emerged (15:1), and it was the "men from James," the half brother of Jesus and leader of the Jerusalem church, that Paul mentions caused so much disruption at Antioch over table fellowship with Gentiles (Gal. 2:12).

On the other hand, we find that the persecutions led the Hellenistic Jews to scatter and spread out in Phoenicia, Cyprus, and Antioch, "speaking the word to no one except Jews" (Acts 11:19). Did Luke mention this detail because he intended his readers to understand the cause of the persecutions and the negative impact it had upon the Hellenistic mission to the Gentiles? Yet Luke notes an amazing turn of events at Antioch—a group of resilient Hellenists decided to preach the gospel to the Gentiles, and the Gentile movement was reignited (11:20). There is a purpose for

---

[47] Grant R. Osborne, *Matthew*, Exegetical Commentary on the New Testament, Clinton E. Arnold, ed. (Grand Rapids, MI: Zondervan, 2010), 599.

Luke's inclusion of this event, and it appears that he intended to contrast the bolder move toward Hellenistic Christianity at Antioch with the more conventional methods at Jerusalem. More than likely, Gentile evangelism continued to retain elements of Torah observance at this stage, but the tremors of its success spread throughout the region and even reached the Jerusalem church. Soon, Barnabas was sent from Jerusalem to see what all the commotion was about and, upon seeing the great things happening at Antioch, went to Tarsus and recruited Saul to help him in the ministry work. How fitting that Saul, the former oppressor of Christians, was now ministering at Antioch, the church he had unwittingly helped to form by his own hand of persecution! It now seemed that all eyes were on Antioch as the Gentile movement was beginning to rumble.

Table Fellowship and the Lord's Supper

Within the scope of table fellowship sat one of the most profound ordinances of early Christian worship—the Lord's Supper. Sacred meals were an integral part of Jewish culture, and it must have been difficult for Jewish Christians to approach Christ's memorial meal with a different perspective. For example, the Jewish fellowship meals such as the Passover and *chaburah*, meals used to inaugurate the Sabbath and on occasions when friends gathered, would have likely been echoed in this sacred meal.[48] A restructuring of the prerequisites was needed for Gentiles as well, who needed to redefine their orientation of what it meant to share a meal—to how Christians were practicing it. Paul addressed these issues in his own writings (1 Cor. 11:17–22, 33–34), ensuring that Gentiles understood the solemnity of the Lord's Supper as a meal of thanksgiving. Of similar importance was determining who was eligible to participate in this divine ordinance now that Torah observance had been set aside. Baptism in Christ now emerged as the new standard of participation in the commemoration of the Last Supper, where "the convert forsakes the Israel that had rejected the Messiah, to join the community that owned

---

[48] Laurie Guy, *Introducing Early Christianity: A Topical Survey of Its Life, Beliefs and Practices* (Downers Grove, IL: InterVarsity Press, 2004), 196.

His sovereignty."[49] It is also no coincidence that the *Didache* was written in Antioch as an instruction guide to Gentiles and instructs that only those baptized in the Lord could participate in the Lord's Supper (*Did.* 9.5). Eventually baptism, as the qualification for participation, became "the standard view of the church."[50]

Despite the new measures now imposed by a new faith in Christ, the foundational problem surrounding Gentile entry into the church was not merely theological but also based on the real and practical problem of table fellowship. How were righteous Jews supposed to sit at the table of fellowship, drink from the same cup, and share the same food, when the Torah specifically forbade such acts? To make matters more difficult, the Christian identification of Jesus as the fulfillment of the Passover Lamb (1 Cor. 5:7–8) immediately recalled God's original requirements for participation in the Passover meal:

> If a stranger shall sojourn with you and would keep the Passover to the Lord, let all his males be circumcised. Then he may come near and keep it; he shall be as a native of the land. But no uncircumcised person shall eat of it. (Exod. 12:48)

It is not a strain to grasp that when the Christian church declared Jesus as the fulfillment of the Passover Lamb, the Jews immediately linked its observance of the Lord's Supper with the OT requirements for the Passover meal. In the midst of this challenge, Paul and the church at Antioch emerged as pioneers in new Jewish-Gentile relations, and particularly within Christ's memorial meal. However, accepting Gentiles freely without regard to the Torah would not be so simple. Indeed, "because of the nature of the Torah's purity laws, Jews were almost bound to regard Gentiles as ritually unclean."[51] Because Jews viewed idolatry as an abomination, and

---

[49] G. R. Beasley-Murray, *Baptism in the New Testament* (Grand Rapids, MI: William B. Eerdmans, 1994), 104.

[50] Guy, 196.

[51] R. H. Stein, "The Jerusalem Church Council," *Dictionary of Paul and His Letters*, Gerald F. Hawthorne, Ralph P. Martin, eds. (Downers Grove, IL: InterVarsity Press, 1993), 336.

Gentiles frequently dedicated food and wine to pagan gods, traditional Jews believed that anyone who "took part in such meals were regarded as apostates."[52]

Even if Gentiles were willing to refrain from food sacrificed to idols, there was still the matter of adhering to stricter Jewish dietary laws and sharing a meal with the uncircumcised. To complicate matters further, some Jews refused to accept Gentiles even if they submitted fully to Judaism as a proselyte! In the midst of this religious milieu, the leaders at Antioch made it standard practice to extend the invitation to Gentiles to share in open table fellowship with uncircumcised Gentiles. What the Hellenists had done in Jerusalem prior to the persecutions now became the standard practice at Antioch (Acts 11:20–24). No longer was the invitation to the Gentiles an exception or an asterisk within the church. It was now abundantly clear, especially at Jerusalem, that a new identity was being forged at the communion table in Antioch.

It may well be that the division between the Aramaic-speaking Jewish "Hebrews" and the Jewish Hellenists, mentioned in Acts 6:1, involved the issue of Gentile contact within the church. Interestingly, the first mention of these two distinct groups is one of dispute, a fact that should not be too quickly overlooked. Because the demarcations made between the two groups of Jews was one of language, possibly two separate synagogue services were observed, since the Greek-speaking Jews would not have been able to attend the Aramaic services.[53] It is also likely that two separate observations of the Blessed Supper were being practiced by each congregation, each with their own unique set of rules for table fellowship pertaining to Gentiles.

Interestingly, the dispute outlined in Acts 6 deals with how the Hellenistic widows were being neglected in the daily distribution of food, an indication that the Hebrews may have been unwilling to serve the Hellenists because the dietary restrictions given in the Torah put them in a compromising position.[54] If the Hebrews' neglecting of the widows

---

[52] Slee, 22.

[53] Ibid., 13.

[54] Philip F. Esler, *Community and Gospel in Luke-Acts: The Social and Political Motivation of Lucan Theology* (Cambridge: Cambridge University Press, 1987), 159–60.

was based on restrictions on table fellowship, then it would explain why the seven men chosen were Hellenists, men who were freely able to serve without table fellowship restrictions. It would also mean that the selection of the first deacons was primarily motivated, not simply to provide table service to the congregation, but to also quell the division that existed between Jewish subgroups. As such, deacons today can take pride in pointing to their origins, not merely as table servers, but as the peacemakers of the church.

An analysis of Galatians 2:11–14 also reveals that the confrontation between Paul and Peter at Antioch was specifically over table fellowship.[55] Paul shares how, when Peter came to Antioch, he sat willingly with the Gentiles in open table fellowship, only to pull away when certain Jews from the Jerusalem church arrived. Paul's descriptive phrase, as "men from James," suggests they had been sent as emissaries by James "to urge the Jewish believers in Antioch to be more careful in their relations with Gentiles."[56] Most certainly, such "care" would point specifically toward table fellowship. Since Peter was already practicing table fellowship with Gentiles before the "men from James" arrived, it means that his motives were not theological but practical. Perhaps Peter was attempting to accommodate the members "whose consciences were scrupulous and unemancipated."[57] Perhaps Peter was seeking peace, not division, in his attempt to appease the visiting Jews in order "to protect the integrity of the Judean mission."[58] However, Paul did not see it that way, understanding that whatever benefits Peter's actions provided the Jewish visitors paled in comparison to the detriments of Jewish-Gentile table fellowship in his treatment of the Gentiles.

---

[55] See the subchapter section entitled "Unrest in Jerusalem" for more discussion on this event.

[56] Leon Morris, *Galatians: Paul's Charter of Christian Freedom* (Downers Grove, IL: InterVarsity Press, 1996), 77.

[57] F. F. Bruce, *Paul: Apostle of the Heart Set Free* (Grand Rapids, MI: William B. Eerdmans, 1993), 177.

[58] Keener, *Galatians,* 164.

The Church at Antioch

When the conflict over the requirements for Gentile admission into the church erupted, the hub of controversy seemed to occur at Antioch. If the Jerusalem church was the center of the Jewish Christian movement, then the Antioch church served as the wellspring of Gentile Christianity. The disciples were first called "Christians" at Antioch (Acts 11:26), another clear indication that they were unique from the predominantly Jewish-Christian communities. It is also worth noting that the term "Christian" (Χριστιανός) was not a word that the members at Antioch used to describe themselves, but rather a derogatory term used by non-Christians.[59] This speaks to the personality of the church at Antioch, whose members had brazenly embraced and lived out the gospel message they had received.

Saul reconnected with the mainstream church at Antioch following his conversion. When the church in Jerusalem received reports of the large number of Gentiles being converted at Antioch, they commissioned Barnabas to go to Antioch (Acts 11:22). Perhaps he was sent to provide encouragement and support to the apostolic work, or perhaps he was charged with ensuring that appropriate table fellowship practices were being observed. Considering that Luke made a point to note that both a great number of conversions occurred at Antioch (11:21) *and* that those conversions occurred precisely when the gospel message turned from strictly Jews (11:19) to the Greeks (11:20), Barnabas likely was commissioned with both duties in mind. After witnessing the great work happening at Antioch, Barnabas sought out Saul in Tarsus to recruit him to assist with the work. One is left to wonder what may have become of Paul if Barnabas had not brought him back into the fold of ministry when he recruited him. If not for the providence of God and Barnabas's faithfulness, Christianity may have been robbed of its greatest Gentile crusader. Within Luke's narrative, the evangelistic work to the Gentiles and the recruitment of Saul by Barnabas highlights Antioch as a major pillar in the life of the early church, drawing "directly and powerfully from Greco-Roman culture as it did from Jewish culture."[60] Thus, in contrast to the church at Jerusalem,

---

[59] Ben Witherington, *The Acts of the Apostles: A Socio-Rhetorical Commentary* (Grand Rapids, MI: William B. Eerdmans, 1998), 751.

[60] Luke Timothy Johnson, *Among the Gentiles: Greco-Roman Religion and*

Antioch appears to occupy a distinguished place in the early Christian church movement because it "refused to be confined within the narrow limits of Judaism."[61]

When the Gentile issue erupted, the churches at Jerusalem and Antioch appeared to stand as pillars on opposing ends of the controversy. When John Mark departed from the first missionary journey, he did not return to Antioch, the site of their departure. Instead, he returned to Jerusalem, where a report was likely given to the leaders at Jerusalem of Paul's activities in Antioch and Asia Minor. One can only appreciate the significance of Mark's return to Jerusalem, and not Antioch, by understanding what each of these churches represented. Is it merely a coincidence that Luke (and Paul) placed Jerusalem and Antioch at odds within John Mark's activities, or did he intend to use Mark's actions as an indicator of the existing cultural chasm that existed between these two churches? Although F. C. Baur's[62] description of a "gulf between Jewish and Gentile Christianity"[63] leaves open the question of just how far-reaching the divide was; the evidence for at least the presence of discord seems apparent. Not only do Paul's letters, and especially Galatians, detail the tension that existed between the two churches, Luke's writing also reveals that the question of Gentile Christian relations was foremost in the minds of its early church leaders.

An important document that displays the varying positions between the churches at Antioch and Jerusalem is the *Didache*, an early second-century manuscript, possibly written in Antioch,[64] that offers basic instructions

---

Christianity, Anchor Yale Bible Reference Library (New Haven, CT: Yale University Press, 2009), 131.

[61] C. H. Thomson, "Antioch" in *The International Standard Bible Encyclopaedia*, James Orr, ed. (Grand Rapids, MI: William B. Eerdmans, 1939), 157.

[62] Ferdinand Christian Baur (1792–1860) was a German Protestant theologian who is perhaps best known as the founder and leader of the Tübingen School of Theology, named for the University of Tübingen, where Baur studied and taught.

[63] Darrell Bock, *Acts*, Baker Exegetical Commentary on the New Testament, Robert W. Yarbrough and Robert H. Stein, eds. (Grand Rapids, MI: Baker Academic, 2007), 520.

[64] Slee, 8. Although Niederwimmer and Attridge argue against Antioch as the origin of the *Didache*, favoring an Egyptian origin, they concede the possibility of Syria-Palestine (the region around Antioch) as the place of origin based on the regional

on baptism and ethics for Gentiles entering the church. Although the manuscript is generally dated to the second century, its sources, at least its "predidachistic traditions," can be reasonably traced back to the first century and the era of the first generation church, "most likely toward the end of the century."[65] The *Didache* is best described as not a "theological" work but a rule for ecclesiastical praxis, a handbook of church morals, ritual, and discipline.[66] Eusebius references the *Didache* as the *"Institutions of the Apostles,"* counting it among the "spurious books" in his canonical list (*Hist. Eccl.* 3.25.4), yet acknowledging that it was "known and approved by many" in the church (3.25.3). The *Didache* reveals that the parties responsible for writing them were opposed by, and themselves oppose, a rival sect within Judaism that insisted on retaining the requirements for Gentile submission to the Torah in order to enter into the covenant community.[67] Indeed, references to table fellowship reflect such opposition, "But let no one eat or drink of this Eucharistic thanksgiving, but they that have been baptized into the name of the Lord; for concerning this also the Lord hath said: Give not that which is holy to the dogs" (9.5).[68] The *Didache* also reveals that, although the Torah was no longer mandatory at Antioch, the Hellenists were still teaching and insisting on Gentile transformation and adherence to the universal Noachic Laws for the purpose of appropriating Jewish-Gentile table fellowship, "But concerning eating, bear that which thou art able; yet abstain by all means from meat sacrificed to idols; for it is the worship of dead gods" (6.3).[69] This teaching appears to reflect James's verdict and instruction to the Gentiles at the Council of Jerusalem (Acts 15:20). If the *Didache* did originate at, or around, the church at Antioch, then it reflects the ecclesiastical superintendence of Antioch, as a church leading the way in Gentile-Christian missions.

---

descriptions (7.2, 9.4) and apostolic presence (11.4–12). See K. Niederwimmer & H. W. Attridge, *The Didache: A Commentary*, Hermeneia (Minneapolis, MN: Fortress Press, 1998), 53.

[65] K. Niederwimmer & H. W. Attridge, *The Didache: A Commentary*, Hermeneia (Minneapolis, MN: Fortress Press, 1998), 52.

[66] Ibid., 2.

[67] Slee, 8.

[68] J. B. Lightfoot and J. R. Harmer, *The Apostolic Fathers* (London: Macmillan, 1891), 232.

[69] Ibid.

The Antioch church plays a major role in Luke's narrative, particularly in the persecution that arises following Stephen's martyrdom. When Stephen (one of the seven original deacons) is stoned by the Jews and a great persecution arises against the church (Acts 8:1), it is primarily the Hellenist Christians, and not the Hebrew Christians, who feel the wrath and flee the persecution. This critical event in the church reveals two factors that must be considered in light of the Jewish-Gentile controversy: (1) The persecution of the Hellenist Jews may have been more about the compromise of the Torah (in the eyes of traditional Jews) in regard to Gentile fellowship than the belief in Jesus as the Messiah and, (2) the dispersion of the Hellenists from Jerusalem may have only served to increase the chasm that already existed between both groups and especially between the church at Jerusalem and those who escaped the persecution and founded the church at Antioch (11:19). From the perspective of the conservative Jews, the Hellenists' open table fellowship with Gentiles may have, in some ways, appeared as the greatest threat to the survival of the Christian church up to that time. After all, if budding Jewish Christianity could defect from Judaism over the person of Christ, then was it possible for Gentile Christianity to break free from Jewish Christianity, if an accord could not be reached? Merrill Tenney[70] captures the urgency of this period masterfully:

> Unless these questions were settled, the relation between Christianity and Judaism would remain unstable, and Christianity would either be abandoned by Judaism, or else two schismatic bodies would be created. One would be the Judaistic church, differing from Judaism only by acknowledging Jesus of Nazareth to be the true Messiah, and the other would be the free Gentile church that would repudiate all the Judaic heritage and become rootless by discarding all previous revelation.[71]

---

[70] Merrill Chapin Tenney (1904–85) was an American professor of NT and Greek at Wheaton College. He also served on the original translation team for the New American Standard Bible and as the second president of the Evangelical Theological Society.

[71] Merrill C. Tenney, *New Testament Times: Understanding the World of the First*

Tenney's point is well taken. In certain ways, a potential ecclesiastical civil war was at stake, and the line in the sand appeared to be the issue of the Gentiles. For the Hellenists who were driven out of Jerusalem and started the church at Antioch, they would have likely gone "beyond the circle of full Jews ... to Gentiles who were interested in Judaism,"[72] placing them in direct opposition to the churches in Jewish Palestine. As the Jerusalem Church continued to root its Christian identity upon the foundations of Judaism, the Antioch Church seemed more progressive in its ambition to embrace the Gentiles.

During this growing controversy, where was John Mark? Mark was native to Jerusalem and brought up in its religious culture (12:12). He was clearly educated in the synagogue and proficient in writing[73] and would have likely attended the Hebrew services. Additionally, his remaining in Jerusalem with the largely "Hebrew" congregation, following the persecution in which Saul was an aggressive participant, gives every indication on what side of the controversy Mark originally stood. It was only a matter of time before Mark's theology sat crossways with Paul's new Gentile schema. It seems the providential hand of God was at work, first scattering the Hellenists and separating them from the dominant "Hebrew" influence of Jerusalem, allowing the churches in both Jerusalem and Antioch to blossom into their own unique identities. It was now time to set Christianity apart from traditional Judaism and fulfill Christ's prophecy: "They will put you out of the synagogues" (John 16:2).

The *Birkat Ha-Minim* and the Early Christian Church

Paul's mission to unite the Jews and Gentiles in a collective movement may have found an unwitting ally when the "Eighteen Benedictions" and the *Birkat Ha-Minim* emerged in the Jewish synagogues during the early

---

Century (Grand Rapids, MI: Baker Books, 2002), 265.

[72] Hengel, 75.

[73] Not only is Mark's Gospel generally regarded to be the product of his work as Peter's amanuensis, but his description as Paul and Barnabas's ὑπηρέτης (assistant) gives indication that his function may have been as one of a more formal capacity, such as record keeper. BDAG, 3rd ed. (Chicago: University of Chicago Press, 2000), 1035.

Christian movement. The "Eighteen Benedictions" is a central prayer that is recited three times a day by all observant Jews while standing, and within this prayer exists the twelfth benediction known as the Birkat Ha-Minim, which curses the *minim* (lit. "kinds"), as heretical sects separated from the righteous.[74] Although archaeological discoveries have unearthed several different versions of the Eighteen Benedictions, of particular interest is the Geniza fragment, the oldest Palestinian witness, which includes among the minim a reference to the *Nazarim* (a specific reference to Christians), known as the "sect of the Nazarenes" (Acts 24:5).[75] Although some scholars argue that the date of the Birkat Ha-Minim should be ascribed to the Council of Yavneh (Jamnia) following the destruction of the temple in AD 70, many scholars believe that the Eighteen Benedictions originated from the Second Temple period and that the main development of the prayer was formed prior to AD 70.[76] Thus, if the curse of the minim (heretics) was expanded to include the "Nazarenes" in Jerusalem, this would indicate that the prayer was amended as a "response to Christianity ... readily employed to reinforce behavior and the boundaries of the community."[77] Within the Geniza fragment, the prayer directs a curse upon the minim and the Nazarim, declaring that they "instantly perish" (T-S K27.33b) and be "blotted from the book of the living."[78] Because the fragment suggests the temple is still standing, and the likely addition of the Nazarim points to a direct cursing of the Christians, a strong case can be made that a "corporate decision"[79] was reached by synagogue leaders to remove the Jews who were confessing Jesus Christ as Messiah. This objective was of such priority in the synagogues that, although other errors in recitation could be overlooked, any errors uttered in the Birkat Haminim required

---

[74] Joel Marcus, "*Birkat Ha-Minim* Revisited," *Journal of New Testament Studies* 55, no. 4 (Oct, 2009): 523–51. doi:http://dx.doi.org.ezproxy.liberty.edu/10.1017/S0028688509990063.

[75] David Instone-Brewer, "The Eighteen Benedictions and the Minim Before 70 CE," *Journal of Theological Studies* 54, no. 1 (April, 2003): 25–44. https://doi-org.ezproxy.liberty.edu/10.1093/jts/54.1.25.

[76] Ibid.

[77] Ruth Langer, *Cursing the Christians? A History of the Birkat Haminim* (New York: Oxford University Press, 2012), 39.

[78] David Instone-Brewer, "The Eighteen Benedictions and the Minim Before 70 CE."

[79] Langer, 27.

repetition in order to ensure a Jew was not a heretic who was deliberately avoiding the utterance. The *Tanhuma Vayiqra*, a halakhic introduction cited in the Jerusalem Talmud, clarified that "if he errs in the *birkat haminim,* we make him repeat and recite it against his will … for if he has some aspect of *minut,* he will curse himself, and the congregation will answer 'amen.'"[80] In other words, although the Jewish synagogue leaders were willing to forgive errors uttered by its congregation on other aspects of this benediction, they would make no such provisions for the Birkat Haminim, lest one of its members is secretly confessing Christ as Messiah and intentionally misreading in order to avoid the curse.

How could such a curse upon Christians be considered an unwitting ally for the Gentile mission? A brief examination of the implications of the curse will reveal two major advantages. First, it is important to remember that Christianity began within the matrix of a Jewish environment and was significantly influenced by Judaism both before and after AD 70.[81] Prior to the Birkat Ha-Minim, the lines of identity were blurred for many Jewish Christians, who attempted to syncretize their newfound faith with their duty to the synagogue. As a result, it was common to see Jewish Christians continuing to fulfill their Sabbath requirements, including attendance in the synagogue. However, the emergence of the Birkat Ha-Minim had marked a definitive line in the sand, forcing Jewish Christians to decide on where their loyalty truly stood. In his analysis of this critical period, Julius Wellhausen, the great German scholar and originator of the "documentary hypothesis,"[82] notes, "For to this period also belongs the definitive separation between the synagogue and the church; henceforward Christianity could no longer figure as a Jewish sect."[83] An example of this very shift may be evident in Acts 18 where Paul goes to Corinth and begins to share the gospel, attempting to persuade both Jews and Greeks (v. 4). After being rejected by the synagogue, Paul declares that he will

---

[80] Ibid., 25.

[81] Guy, 194.

[82] Julius Wellhausen (1844–1918), was a German biblical scholar and one of few who have profoundly impacted both NT and OT studies. He served as professor at the Universities of Göttingen, Greifswald, Halle and Marburg.

[83] Julius Wellhausen, *Prolegomena to the History of Ancient Israel* (Cambridge: Cambridge University Press, 2013), 574.

now go to the Gentiles (Acts 13:46, 18:6), and moves next door to the home of the Gentile, Titius Justus, where he establishes the home church at Corinth. It would thus appear that the Birkat Ha-Minim would push Jewish Christians away from the synagogue and into closer fellowship with their Gentile brethren. If the benediction and curse were intended to "weld the whole of Judaism into a monolithic structure"[84] by removing Christians and/or any other threat to orthodoxy, then perhaps it unwittingly forged Christianity into a more solid identity as well. Now, all doubt as to spiritual identity would be removed, as Jewish Christians, as well as Gentiles, would be united under the banner of Christ by faith. Simply put, Jewish Christians now realized a stronger bond with their Gentile brethren than the Jews who had ousted them from the synagogues.

The second advantage would be found in that the curse acknowledged Christianity as a legitimate threat and primary target as the "*minim par excellence*" against the synagogue.[85] This now meant that the synagogue had begun "to view the Christian movement as an essential and more or less clearly distinguishable rival."[86] No longer did the Christian movement need to be confined to the synagogue as the target of its gospel. To the benefit of the Christian church, and especially the Gentiles, the new mission would now follow the edict of the Jerusalem Council and begin to move beyond the Jewish synagogue. J. Louis Martyn, one of the leading pioneers in Johannine research,[87] identified three passages in the Gospel of John that he believed referred to the Birkat Ha-Minim, and suggests that in each case a clear reference to the decision of the Jamnia Academy is evident. In John 9:22, John offers an "aside"[88] in his narrative on the

---

[84] J. Louis Martyn, *History and Theology in the Fourth Gospel*. 3rd ed. (Louisville, KY: Westminister John Knox Press, 2003), 63.

[85] Joel Marcus, "*Birkat Ha-Minim* Revisited."

[86] Martyn, 47.

[87] J. Louis Martyn (1925–2015) is widely recognized as a leading scholar in Johannine and Pauline studies. He served as professor at Union Theological Seminary (NYC), where he became Edward Robinson Professor of Biblical Theology in 1967, a post he held until his retirement in 1987. His contribution to this particular perspective on the Birkat Ha-Minim in John's Gospel changed the face of Johannine studies for decades.

[88] Köstenberger notes the importance of John's use of "asides" in order to clarify issues and/or provide information on certain aspects of his narrative. In this case,

blind man healed by Jesus, noting that the parents of the blind man were afraid to respond to the Pharisees, "for the Jews *had already agreed* that if anyone should confess Jesus to be Christ, he was to be put out of the synagogue."[89] Again, John shares how many of the Jewish leaders believed in Jesus but refused to confess because of their fear that they would be "put out of the synagogue" (12:42). In John 16:2, even Jesus warns His disciples, "They will put you out of the synagogues." Martyn believed that John made direct reference to the Benediction prayer that was apparently reformulated to include the Nazarim (Christians) amongst the minim (heretics) as a "means for detecting those Jews who want to hold a dual allegiance to Moses and to Jesus as Messiah ... to separate such Jews from the synagogue."[90] Although Martyn's theory is plausible, the Benediction prayers seemed to be a common practice for all kinds of reasons.

In the later years following the destruction of the Jerusalem temple in AD 70, the Council at Jamnia (*bet-din*, lit. "house of judgment"), succeeded the former Sanhedrin at Jerusalem and became the "administrative seat of Jewish life."[91] In many ways, the decree made at Jamnia to oust the Christians from the synagogue reflects an earlier tradition that may have emerged when Paul began to methodically preach Jesus as the Messiah within the synagogues. This expulsion may have unwittingly united Christian Jews and Gentiles in a stronger cause for Christ. Ferguson notes that the "Jamnia period marks the beginning of the change from a temple-oriented Judaism comprising a variety of sects to a more united Judaism centered around the local synagogues."[92] One could argue that a similar

---

John may be using this aside in order to offer background information pertaining to the Council of Jamnia's decision to oust Christians from the synagogue. Andreas J. Köstenberger, *Encountering John: The Gospel in Historical, Literary, and Theological Perspective*, 2nd ed. (Grand Rapids, MI: Baker Academic, 2013), 231.

[89] Although a general consensus on the exact date of Christian expulsion from the Jewish synagogues may never be reached, the absence of a Johannine explanation or commentary in this text may reveal principles of intertextuality at work and further proof that Christian expulsion from the synagogues in the Syro-Palestinian region had already transpired.

[90] Martyn, 66.

[91] Everett Ferguson, *Backgrounds of Early Christianity*, 2nd ed. (Grand Rapids, MI: William B. Eerdmans, 1993), 400.

[92] Ibid.

unified front within Christianity may have resulted between Christian Jews and Gentiles identified by faith in Christ. If so, then it happened at the Jerusalem Council. As the church at Antioch prospered, the church at Jerusalem now stood firmly on its own, apart from the Jewish temple. The stage was now set to inspire and endorse the new Gentile mission in the same way that the Lord had initiated the Jewish Christian church—by the seal of the Holy Spirit.

The Cornelius Event

Luke's account of the conversion of Cornelius, the Roman centurion at Caesarea, is so strategically well-positioned within the narrative of Acts that it is difficult to ignore the multiplicity of literary clues that it contributes to the Gentile salvation story. Although Cornelius is not the first Gentile convert accepted without first being circumcised (Acts 8:26–40), this event leads Peter and the Jerusalem church to officially accept "an uncircumcised Gentile into God's covenant people."[93] Prior to the Cornelius event, the story of Acts seems to carry the Gentile issue as a tense undercurrent beneath the flow of activities happening within the Christian community. Immediately afterward, the Gentile story seems to burst forth, as the Antioch church comes to the forefront, and Saul and Barnabas are commissioned on their first missionary journey. Luke may have intended to use the conversion of Cornelius as an apology that would be later used at the Jerusalem Council "as decisive evidence of the acceptance of the Gentiles by God."[94] Indeed, it would appear that the key issue within the Cornelius story centers around Gentile eligibility and the need to set aside old Jewish prejudices, "especially those relating to particularism and privilege within Christianity."[95] Thus, the Cornelius story serves as the key event that shifts the flow of Luke's narrative and brings the Gentile issue to front and center stage in three distinct ways: (1)

[93] Craig S. Keener, *Acts: An Exegetical Commentary*, vol. 2 (Grand Rapids, MI: Baker Academic, 2013), 1727.

[94] Martin Dibelius, *Studies in the Acts of the Apostles*, Heinrich Greeven, ed. (Mifflintown, PA: Sigler Press, 1999), 109.

[95] J. Julius Scott Jr., *"The Cornelius Incident in the Light of its Jewish Setting," Journal of Evangelical Theological Society* 34, no. 4 (December 1991), 475–84.

God's election of Peter to authorize and experience the Cornelius event, (2) the Jerusalem church's acceptance of Peter's testimony and new doctrine toward Gentiles, and (3) the reception of the Holy Spirit and resulting glossolalia for the Gentiles at Caesarea.

1. God's Election of Peter to Authorize and Experience the Cornelius Event

Of all the possible candidates, God elected Peter, the key apostle to the Jews, as the recipient of the divine vision that would make Gentile table fellowship possible. Peter was also led by the Holy Spirit to preach to Cornelius and his household and witness firsthand the reception of the Holy Spirit by the Gentiles. While Saul ministered in Tarsus and Cilicia during his "silent years," God was already laying the groundwork for the Gentile mission by calling Peter to adopt a new global mission. It is difficult to imagine a more perfect candidate to receive this divine vision and witness the adoption of the Gentiles into the kingdom of God firsthand. This man, whom Jesus called "the Rock" (Matt. 16:18), would become the face of the church at Jerusalem and a primary apostle commissioned to the "circumcised" (Gal. 2:7). He was also a man with the eyes and ears to receive God's Word and the heart to accept it. Of Peter's many flaws, one of his greatest virtues was his capacity for self-examination and willingness to rethink his attitude. At Caesarea Philippi he was challenged to rethink the Messiah's mission (Matt. 16:21–23). After his thrice-denial of Christ, Peter was forced to reconsider his loyalty to Christ (Lk. 22:54–62), and after his reinstatement by Christ on the shores of Galilee, this humble fisherman seemed poised to embrace a renewed devotion to his ministry (John 21:15–19). Though Peter seemed intent on evangelizing strictly to the Jews up until this event, he was led by divine guidance to preach to Cornelius, a Gentile "Godfearer" (Acts 10:22), and his household. However, before his unprecedented mission, a divine revelation was first needed in order to prepare him to perform his task without restraint.

While praying on a rooftop in Joppa, the apostle witnessed a vision of both kosher and non-kosher foods brought down on a sheet from heaven and a voice instructing him to "kill and eat" (Acts 10:13). Despite his initial protests, Peter was told that God had now cleansed what was once common (10:15).[96] Although the vision served as reference to Jewish food restrictions, he was able to discern that "its range is much wider,"[97] when he later tells Cornelius, "God has shown me that I should not call any *person* common or unclean" (10:28). In the broader vision, he was able to understand that "it is men and women, even Gentiles, whose hearts [Christ] has cleansed by faith."[98] Undoubtedly, Peter's experience had much to do with his willingness to embrace the new, liberated mission to the Gentiles. God's selection of Joppa as the city where Peter received the divine vision is intriguing, for it connects him with an OT prophet who also received a vision for the Gentiles—Jonah. At Joppa, Jonah boarded a ship to flee from God's call to bring salvation to the Gentiles (Jonah 1:3). Where Jonah failed, Peter readily embraced his call at Joppa to bring the gospel to the Gentiles. Later, the enlightened apostle specifically referenced the Cornelius event at the Jerusalem Council as evidence for his endorsement of Paul and Barnabas's new commission to the Gentiles (Acts 15:7–11). From the perspective of John Mark, Peter's change toward the Gentile mission would have been significant. It would certainly have been humbling for Mark to witness his mentor's endorsement of Paul's mission at the Jerusalem Council and to realize his prior actions at Pamphylia had stood in direct contrast.

2. The Jerusalem Church's Acceptance of Peter's Testimony and New Doctrine toward Gentiles

After his vision at Joppa and witness of the pouring out of the Holy Spirit upon the Gentiles, Peter returned to Jerusalem, where he was "criticized" (διακρίνω) by the "circumcision party" (Acts 11:2).[99] They had taken issue with Peter because he had done something that, up to that point, had not

---

[96] The aorist active indicative of καθαρίζω, "to cleanse," indicates that what was once unclean has now been cleansed by God.

[97] F. F. Bruce, *The Book of Acts,* The New International Commentary on the New Testament, rev. ed. Gordon D. Fee, ed. (Grand Rapids, MI: William B. Eerdmans, 1988), 206.

[98] Ibid.

[99] See subchapter entitled "Hebrews" and "Hellenists" for more information on the "circumcision party."

been done in the Jerusalem church: "You went to uncircumcised men and ate with them" (v. 3). Table fellowship was the key point of contention for this group—the sharing of a meal with uncircumcised Gentiles. It is interesting that the Jews took issue with Peter's table fellowship and yet made no mention about their being baptized. This illustrates that "table fellowship and acceptance of the Gentiles were closely related,"[100] and that Peter's shared meal with the Gentiles demonstrated his acceptance of them as fellow Christians, although they were still uncircumcised. Luke's account of Peter's vision and encounter with Cornelius appeared to be aimed less at the preaching to the Gentiles, per se, and more at the open table fellowship between Jew and Gentile now made available by God. Thus, when the apostle gave an account to the "circumcision group," who questioned his table fellowship with Gentiles, Luke aimed to show that Peter's actions were controversial, not because he preached to Gentiles, but because "he dares to share a meal with them."[101] He offered a summary of the events that unfolded, including his vision at Joppa and his witnessing of their reception of the Holy Spirit after receiving the gospel message. After hearing his report to the church, the "circumcision party" seemingly agreed and accepted this new doctrine toward the Gentiles.

Where was John Mark during this transformative event? Although possibly he was still in Jerusalem at this time, it is also feasible that Mark was already serving with his cousin Barnabas at Antioch and had not heard about what had transpired with Peter (Acts 11:22, 12:25). Up until this time, Peter had clearly not practiced table fellowship with Gentiles (10:28), so the events at Antioch most likely occurred afterward (Gal. 2:11–14). Thus, it seems best to place the Cornelius event immediately prior to Peter's visit to Antioch, where he initially practiced table fellowship with the Gentiles and then withdrew when the "circumcision party" arrived from Jerusalem. Mark possibly was present at Antioch during the confrontation outlined in Galatians 2:11–14. However, it is more likely that he was in Jerusalem, where he heard about Peter's report about the

---

[100] John B. Polhill, *Acts*, The New American Commentary, vol. 26, Edited by David S. Dockery (Nashville, TN: B&H Publishing, 1992), 266.

[101] Ivor J. Davidson, *The Birth of the Church: From Jesus to Constantine*, The Baker History of the Church, vol. 1, Tim Dowley, ed. (Grand Rapids, MI: Baker Books, 2004), 62.

events surrounding Cornelius. If so, then he either rejected the majority decision of the Jerusalem church (an unlikely premise) or stood with those who were willing to accept the uncircumcised Gentiles into the church but were not yet willing to practice table fellowship with them. This is not totally unreasonable, for even Peter struggled to put into practice that which he received directly from the Holy Spirit (2:12). Additionally, if the Gentile issue had been settled after Peter's report to the Jerusalem church, then it would not have erupted later at Antioch (Acts 15:1) or served as the focus of debate at the Jerusalem Council (15:5).

3. The Reception of the Holy Spirit and Resulting Glossolalia for the Gentiles at Caesarea

Much has been made of the reception of the Holy Spirit and the resulting glossolalia (speaking in tongues) that followed, both at Pentecost (Acts 2:1–4) and at Caesarea (10:44–48). Although space eludes us here for a more thorough discussion of this phenomenon, the details surrounding the reception of the Holy Spirit at both Pentecost and Caesarea as it pertains to the Gentile mission is both relevant and insightful.[102] Indeed, theological paradigms have been built around these two events, resulting in doctrines that accept glossolalia as evidence of the reception of the Holy Spirit and a symbol that it is a spiritual gift that is still active today. However, when one examines these events, as Luke likely intended them for his original audience, two major ecclesiastical misapplications become evident.

First, the Greek term "tongues" (*glōssa*) describes "a body of words and systems that makes up a distinctive language."[103] Thus, the basis of the miracles described in Acts 2 and 10 was found specifically in the miraculous ability to speak a previously unknown *distinctive language* and one that was also clearly understood and interpreted by its witnesses.[104]

---

[102] For more thorough discussion on this subject, see James D. G. Dunn, *Baptism in the Holy Spirit: A Re-examination of the New Testament Teaching on the Gift of the Spirit in Relation to Pentecostalism Today* (Philadelphia: Westminister Press, 1970).
[103] BDAG, 3rd ed., 201.
[104] This definition differs wildly from the "ecstatic speech" that is seen and practiced in many charismatic and Pentecostal churches today, which lacks miraculous power and the required interpretive witness (1 Cor. 14:28).

The power behind the event was in that those who spoke in tongues were understood by the hearers, "so that God's word is proclaimed in a comprehensible manner."[105] Second, of the Lukan witness to people "filled with the Holy Spirit," only a handful result in glossolalia (Acts 2:1–4, 10:44–48, 19:1–7). Thus, it is evident that one's being filled with the Holy Spirit does not necessitate the speaking in tongues. The first Lukan account of a person being filled with the Holy Spirit occurs in Luke 1:41, when Elizabeth was filled with the Holy Spirit after hearing Mary's greeting. Elizabeth rejoices but does not speak in tongues. This passage is hermeneutically significant because the first account in a biblical text usually serves as the prototype for doctrinal formation.[106] Why, then, should the two accounts of persons speaking in tongues, when filled with the Holy Spirit, serve as the basis for such doctrine when it neither stands as the prototype nor as the predominant witness to the NT?

When John the Baptist is born, his father Zechariah is filled with the Holy Spirit and begins to prophesy but does not speak in tongues (Lk. 1:67). Simeon, who was promised by the Holy Spirit that he would not see death until he looked upon the newborn Christ, is filled with the Spirit when he blesses the child and yet never utters a foreign word (2:25–32). When Saul receives Christ and is healed by Ananias, he is filled with the Holy Spirit, and the scales from his eyes fall off, but he does not engage in glossolalia (Acts 9:17–18). Again, when Paul is in Cyprus, he is filled with the Holy Spirit when he confronts Elymas the magician and blinds him but does not make any declarations outside his native tongue (13:8–12). When Peter speaks before the Temple Council after his arrest, he is filled with the Holy Spirit and boldly preaches Christ but does not voice an alien language (4:8). When the church receives Peter's and John's report, they are all filled with the Holy Spirit and continue "to speak the word of God with boldness" (4:31) but do not speak in tongues. Thus, it seems apparent that the charisma of speaking in tongues should not stand as the basis for

---

[105] Thomas R. Schreiner, *New Testament Theology: Magnifying God in Christ* (Grand Rapids, MI: Baker Academic, 2008), 444.

[106] Many thanks to Dr. Rudy Gonzalez for this insightful contribution to my research.

the reception of the Holy Spirit or that the gift of speaking in tongues is now available to any who ask for it. Frederick Dale Bruner[107] aptly notes:

> The absence of the *seeking* of the speaking in tongues is significant. It, with the intelligibility of the tongues, places seriously in question the adequacy of Pentecost as a "pattern" for the Pentecostal baptism in the Holy Spirit ... However, neither in Acts 2 nor in Acts 8, 10, or 19—the primary Pentecostal texts for tongues as evidence—are tongues recorded as *sought.* Thus, there is an internal contradiction in the creedal use of Acts 2:4 in each *Pentecostal Evangel,* the major American Pentecostal journal: "We believe that the Baptism of the Holy Spirit according to Acts 2:4 is given to believers who ask for it." For the tongues-baptism in the Holy Spirit, according to Acts 2:4, is not asked for. In fact, in neither Acts 2, Acts 8 (where no tongues are recorded at all), Acts 10, nor Acts 19 is either a baptism in the Holy Spirit *or* speaking in tongues asked for by the recipients. Must this not affect the Pentecostal doctrine of a specifically sought baptism in the Holy Spirit with its evidence of tongues?[108]

If the biblical evidence demonstrates that glossolalia is not universally endorsed in scripture as a requisite for possession of the Holy Spirit, then what meaning did Luke intend for the events outlined in Acts 2:1–4 and 10:44–48? Is it possible that these two unique accounts were meant to serve a specific theological purpose for Luke's readers?[109] As has been

---

[107] Frederick Dale Bruner (born 1932), is a missionary and theologian who has devoted much of his work to the strengthening of church doctrine. His book, *A Theology of the Holy Spirit: The Pentecostal Experience and the New Testament Witness,* is a critical examination of Pentecostal theology and insightful resource on the subject.

[108] Frederick Dale Bruner, *A Theology of the Holy Spirit: The Pentecostal Experience and the New Testament Witness* (Unicoi, TN: Trinity Foundation, 2001), 164–65.

[109] The only other Lukan account of divine speech in Acts 19:1–7 seems less problematic, for it clearly is intended to teach the disciples at Ephesus the difference between the baptism of John the Baptist and Jesus Christ.

clearly argued, these two accounts cannot mean that the Holy Spirit was authenticating His presence for all those to bear witness, for it would otherwise invalidate all other accounts in which reception of the Spirit did not result in such miraculous speech. Perhaps the better question is what was Luke trying to tell us by demonstrating that the Holy Spirit elected these two specific events as the sites to demonstrate the miracle of tongues? What did these two events have in common, and what set them apart? In both events, we witness the initial reception of the Holy Spirit, and yet what distinguishes them from each other are the specific people that are blessed. On the Day of Pentecost, it is the Jews who are introduced to the third member of the Holy Trinity, who commissions the new church among the Jews that acknowledge Jesus Christ as Messiah. In the Cornelius event, it is the Gentiles who are now sanctioned by the Holy Spirit in order to validate them as eligible members to receive Christian baptism and enter into the fellowship of the Christian community, apart from circumcision or any other observation of Mosaic Law. It is a proleptic argument for Israel, and one that Luke anticipated within the Jewish community. Thus, the arrival and reception of the Holy Spirit, including its resulting miracle of glossolalia, was meant to serve as a divine endorsement of its recipients as the true church (ekklēsia) of God, first for the Jew (2:1–4), then for the Gentile (10:44–48).

Why did God elect the miracle of languages as the means of demonstrating His divine approval of both the Jewish and Gentile causes? The answer can be traced back to Genesis and the account of the Tower of Babel. As humans, in their great pride, attempt to build a tower that reaches the heavens in order to make a great name for themselves, God confuses their language in order to disperse them (Gen. 11:1–9). What results is a scattering of people who will remain divided by tongue and ethnic identity. At Pentecost, that curse is reversed when the Holy Spirit empowers humanity with the supernatural ability to supersede the confusing elements of speech and now speak the universal language of Jesus Christ (Acts 2:1–11). Humans, once divided over pride and desire for self-deification, are once again reunited as one people, one nation, and one tongue in Jesus Christ: "That damaging confusion and devastating destruction is reversed at Pentecost ... The Spirit alters the effects of their languages from deconstructing the community to reconstructing the new community of the church ... Filled with the Holy Spirit, we hear, understand, and sacrifice in love for one another."[110]

Much to Peter's surprise, when he preached the gospel to Cornelius and his household, the Holy Spirit befell its recipients, and they began to speak in tongues and prophesy in the same way as the Jews at Pentecost (Acts 10:46–47). Peter immediately recognized its meaning as God's approval of the Gentiles into the kingdom of God, and commanded that they be baptized "in the name of Jesus" without the requirement of circumcision (10:48). The church today would do well to adopt Peter's interpretation, "not primarily to denote empowering for charismatic ministry but rather to signify that those who received the Spirit belonged to the people of God."[111] The reception of the Holy Spirit by Cornelius's household mirrors the events at Pentecost and demonstrates God's approval of the Gentiles apart from the requirements of circumcision and adherence to the Torah. Thus, it seems that the most proper way to interpret the miracle of speaking in tongues, both at Pentecost and in the Cornelius event, should be, not as the modus operandi for the reception of the Holy Spirit today, but as God's endorsement of both the Jews and Gentiles as eligible members of the Christian covenant community. The human language, once scattered at Babel, was once again reunited by the power of the Holy Spirit. Luke uses the Cornelius event in order to set the stage for the great Gentile story that emerges, along with the introduction of one of its great characters— John Mark.

---

[110] Bruce K. Waltke, *Genesis: A Commentary* (Grand Rapids, MI: Zondervan, 2001), 184.

[111] Schreiner, *New Testament Theology*, 454.

CHAPTER 3

JOHN MARK ENTERS
THE NARRATIVE

*O*ne of the majestic aspects of Luke's writing style is his timing. At the macro level, the "presentation of the time of the church in Acts is extraordinarily realistic."[112] The Sitz Im Leben of the early Christian church comes to life at the tip of Luke's pen. At the micro level, it is as if, at every turn, a key character, witness, or event enters the scene with harmonious precision. For example, after Paul and Barnabas separate over the issue of Mark, Silas joins Paul on the second journey, as if to replace Barnabas. Later, when they arrive at Lystra, Timothy enters the scene and is recruited by Paul, as if to fill the void left behind by Mark (Acts 16:1). Another example is found in Acts 16:10 where, after Paul receives his vision of the man from Macedonia, Luke seamlessly shifts from third person to first person in order to demonstrate that he has now joined the missionary group. The timing of John Mark is no different.

At first, Mark appears in the background of the narrative as an ancillary character. His first mention is made only as a casual description of his mother's house to which Peter ran after his miraculous escape from prison (Acts 12:12). Afterward, he appears in a supporting role for Barnabas and Paul, both at Antioch (12:25) and when they set sail for Cyprus on the first excursion into the Roman provinces of Asia Minor (13:5). Only when Mark abandons the mission at Perga does the reader begin to sit

---

[112] Norman Perrin and Dennis C. Duling, *The New Testament: An Introduction*, 2nd ed. (San Diego, CA: Harcourt Brace Jovanovich, 1982), 307.

up and take notice. Something noteworthy has occurred here, and yet Luke's silence seems deafening. Yet, after Mark returns to Jerusalem, it seems an odd and timely coincidence that members of the Jerusalem church intentionally make their way to Antioch in order to teach and insist that the Gentiles be circumcised for their own salvation (15:1). What sparked this group to action? Luke does not tell us if Mark was among this crowd, but the dissension that erupts between Paul and Barnabas and the "circumcision group" is of sufficient magnitude that a small committee is formed to go to Jerusalem in order to resolve the issue (15:2). Only after the Jerusalem Council is Luke's silence, left lingering at Perga, now broken. The resulting split between Paul and Barnabas over Mark's eligibility to once again accompany them leaves the reader with no doubt that Mark's actions have indeed held serious implications (15:37–39), but thanks be to God that Mark's story does not end here! Although Mark's actions had bruised some relationships, Mark presses on with his cousin toward Cypress and continues his ministry. He reunites with Peter and eventually even with Paul. He serves both men and never again does Mark seem to disappoint in the ministry. At the end of Paul's life, we find that Mark has become a most "useful" (εὔχρηστος) servant (2 Tim. 4:11), as does Peter, whom he has always considered a son (1 Pet. 5:13).

What then are we to make of Luke's characterization of John Mark? What macro-function does Mark play in the stream of this storyline? Our understanding of John Mark must acknowledge that characters "are constructs of the implied author, created to fulfill a particular role in the story ... whose existence sometimes transcends the purpose for which they are created."[113] Thus, from a narrative-critical perspective, John Mark is representative of the reluctant Jewish Christian who initially hesitates to accept the Gentiles, but is eventually won over by the work of the Holy Spirit and comes to embrace the new Gentile mission. He is discipled under Peter's wing, in his mother's household, growing in the knowledge of Christ. He works silently behind Paul and Barnabas, watching and learning. With great enthusiasm, he joins Saul and Barnabas on the way to Cyprus and begins to witness the power of the Holy Spirit on that island. Although the most impressive conversion at Cyprus was

---

[113] Mark Allan Powell, *What is Narrative Criticism?* (Minneapolis, MN: Fortress Press, 1990), 52.

Sergius Paulus, a Gentile, Mark is not ready to embrace a direct mission to Gentiles. As the trio sailed from Cyprus to Pamphylia, Paul made a stunning announcement—the way to the Gentiles had now been opened by the Holy Spirit, and he had been called to lead the charge. It was time for Israel to become the light to the nations that Isaiah had long ago prophesied (Isa. 42:6). Mark may have sat on the edge of the boat, eyeing the shores ahead and wondering if he could really be the man Paul was challenging him to be. Was he ready for such a radial mission? Sadly, on the shores of Perga, Mark decides to board a ship returning to Jerusalem, in quiet protest of Paul's new Gentile agenda. With possible great confliction, Mark offers his report to the Jerusalem church and watches the controversy unfold. Later, he receives Paul and Barnabas at the Jerusalem Council with tension, knowing that Paul was left disappointed. Mark sits quietly in the background of the Jerusalem Council, listening intently as the reports are given and the hand of fellowship is offered by the Jerusalem church. He is humbled by Peter's testimony of his vision at Joppa and witness of the Holy Spirit falling upon the uncircumcised Gentiles. After hearing Peter's endorsements, Mark surrenders his final prejudices when James, the leader of the Jerusalem church, renders his final verdict in full support of the new Gentile mission. With a renewed conviction, Mark is ready to rejoin Paul and Barnabas. However, Paul's wounds would need time to heal, and in the meantime, Mark assists his cousin Barnabas in his work in Cyprus. Over the course of several years, Mark would prove himself a changed man. The Jewish Christian who, at one time could not bring himself to sit at the same table with an uncircumcised Gentile, had now fully embraced the Gentiles and had once again been made "useful" (εὔχρηστος) for the church. Eventually, Mark pens the Gospel that the world now acknowledges as the Gospel for the Gentiles.

For some, such a character representation of Mark may seem too presumptuous. However, the implied author does not always reveal characters by telling the reader directly about them. Rather, the author often goes "beneath the surface of the action to obtain a reliable view of a character's mind and heart,"[114] by showing the reader what the characters are like within the story itself. Indeed, Luke often lays out the facts of each

---

[114] Wayne C. Booth, *Rhetoric of Fiction*, 2nd ed. (Chicago: University of Chicago Press, 1983), 3.

event and "leaves the reader to gather for himself the causal connection between them."[115] Through this lens, Mark's transformation speaks for itself, and Luke may have intended for his character to reflect his hope that all Jewish Christians could follow suit. Many Jewish Christians in Luke's day would have identified and sympathized with Mark, and possibly Luke fully intended for Mark's character to represent the transformative journey that all Jewish believers must undertake if they too wish to be made "useful" for the new Christian movement. This truth persists in the life of the church today, as Christians are also challenged to cast away their own prejudices before being made effective for God's ministry. Despite Mark's shortcomings, Luke believed that Mark could change,[116] and this was his hope for the church. In the end, we should not be too quick to assume that Luke did not leave clear evidence of this transformative process at work in the life of Mark. Indeed, Luke left vibrant textual clues, and none more powerful than in his use of Mark's name.

What's in a Name? Textual Clues in Luke's Narrative

Silence, in certain contexts, does not always imply that a historian has nothing to say. Indeed, Hengel notes that where Luke is silent about something, "there are usually special reasons for it."[117] Despite Luke's silence on the motivation behind John Mark's departure, several clues are seemingly in place within the narrative, including word structure, the use of names, name order, and the sequence of events surrounding John Mark's departure. It is worth noting that Luke varies the use of John Mark's name, differentiating the Hebrew name "John" and the Gentile (Roman) name "Mark" throughout his narrative. When paralleled with the events surrounding Mark's departure from the mission in Acts 13:13, the pattern becomes even more striking. As such, Luke's use of Mark's name can be categorized in four ways: (1) "John, whose other name was Mark" (12:12, 25); (2) only "John" (13:5, 13); (3) "John called Mark" (15:37); and (4)

---

[115] William M. Ramsay, *St. Paul: The Traveler and Roman Citizen*, Mark Wilson, ed. (Grand Rapids, MI: Kregel Publications, 2001), 85.

[116] Keener, *Acts,* 2031.

[117] Hengel, 36.

only "Mark" (15:39). Let us explore each of these name patterns in greater detail.

1. "John, whose other name was Mark" (Acts 12:12, 25)

The first reference Luke makes of Mark is as "John, whose other name was Mark" (Acts 12:12). This is significant because it serves as an indicator of how Luke wants to introduce Mark to his readers. During this introduction, Mark is at his mother's house in Jerusalem, most likely a home church, praying for the release of Peter with other Christians (Acts 12:12). He is under Peter's guidance, a man called primarily to the Jews (Gal. 2:7). Mark was also the cousin of Barnabas (Col. 4:10), a Levite and native of Cyprus (Acts 4:36), and a man of rank in the Jerusalem church (11:22–24). Although Luke refers to Mark by both names at this opening stage, he does not use the simple combination of "John Mark." It is often overlooked that the Hebrew name "John" (Ἰωάννης) is given priority over his Gentile name of "Mark" (Μᾶρκος). This again occurs in his second reference, when Peter and Barnabas return to Antioch from Jerusalem and take along with them "John, whose other name was Mark" (12:25). In both of these references, Luke applies the participle form of ἐπικαλέω to identify John's Gentile name of Mark as merely "a surname."[118] It is as if Luke intends to imply that, at this initial stage, although John Mark possesses both a Hebrew and Gentile identity, his self-identity is primarily Hebrew.

2. "John" (Acts 13:5, 13)

When Paul, Barnabas, and Mark depart from Antioch on their first mission into Asia, Luke refers to Mark only by his Hebrew name of "John," noting that Paul and Barnabas "had John to assist them" (Acts 13:5). When Mark departs from the mission at Perga, he again is referred to only as "John," who "left them and returned to Jerusalem" (13:13). It is striking that, of the only two times that Luke identifies John Mark as simply "John," it is at the start of the first Pauline missionary journey and at the lowest point of his ministerial career—his departure from that

---

[118] BDAG, 3rd ed., 373.

same mission. It is as if Luke means to say that, at these critical junctures, Mark is a man who thinks and acts only by his Hebrew identity and thus is not yet ready to embrace the Gentile initiative. The Gentile person of "Mark" is nowhere to be found. Only the Hebrew "John" is thinking and acting in these moments. Interestingly, Adolf Deissmann, one of the great German Greek scholars of the twentieth century, admits that Luke's usage of the single name "John" (Ἰωάννης) in Acts 13:13 "has been used purposely" but then suggests that his usage of only "Mark" in Acts 15:39 "may be accidental or on purpose."[119] Luke would not be so inconsistent. The textual evidence seems to favor both a design and an intentionality behind this phenomenon.

3. "John called Mark" (Acts 15:37)

After the Jerusalem Council, when Paul and Barnabas decide to return on a second mission, Barnabas again desires to take John Mark with them, but this time Luke refers to Mark by the slightly modified form, "John called Mark" (Acts 15:37). This does not mirror his earlier dual reference to both names (12:12, 25). Here, Luke uses the participle form of καλέω, which indicates that the individual here is "called by, addressed as, or designated" by both names.[120] In other words, the Hebrew name John (Ἰωάννης) here no longer appears to hold priority of identity since he is now equally identified by both names. It is as if Luke intends to demonstrate that, since the time of his departure from the first mission, Mark's identity has experienced another significant transformation—he now identifies with both the Hebrew and Gentile causes. Perhaps here, Luke means to illustrate that John Mark had accepted the testimony of his mentor, Peter (Acts 15:7–11) and the decision of the Jerusalem Council to embrace the Gentiles without the requirements of adopting Jewish customs.

4. "Mark" (Acts 15:39; Col. 4:10; Philem. 1:24; 2 Tim. 4:11; 1 Pet. 5:13)

Perhaps most striking is the name change that occurs after John Mark departs with his cousin Barnabas back to Cyprus (Acts 15:39). After this

---

[119] G. Adolf Deissmann, *Bible Studies* (Charleston, SC: BiblioBazaar, 2010), 317.
[120] BDAG, 3rd ed., 502.

point, Mark will be acknowledged only by his Gentile name of "Mark" by all who reference him, including Luke, Paul (Col. 4:10; Philem. 1:24; 2 Tim. 4:11), and even Peter (1 Pet. 5:13). It is as if Luke intends to demonstrate that Mark's spiritual transformation is now complete and affirmed by all who colabor with him. This is not to suggest that Mark cast away his Jewishness because the single name of "John" is no longer used. Luke means to say that the name "Mark" encompasses both identities, for the door between Jews and Gentiles was never shut on the part of the Gentiles. The *metamorphoō* has forged Mark into a man who now fully embraces Christ's mission to Jew and Gentile alike. From this perspective, Luke's use of Mark's name does not appear random but rather intentional, reflecting the theological transformation occurring over the course of his life and ministry.

If Luke's literary use of different Markan name formulas was not intended to represent such a transformative process, then one must account for these variations. It would seem less reasonable to assume that Luke used such name patterns for his characters randomly. Similar patterns are also evident in Luke's use of Paul's name, who was born a Roman citizen with both his Hebrew name of "Saul" and Roman name of "Paul."[121] Luke also appears to strategically use Paul's names within his chronicle with clear authorial intent. Although it may seem most logical that Luke would shift Saul's name to "Paul" after his encounter with Jesus on the road to Damascus (Acts 9), Luke withholds the transfer of names until Acts 13:13, exactly when John Mark departs at Perga and Paul begins his Gentile ministry. At this juncture Paul initiates his ministry to the Gentiles at Pisidian Antioch (13:46). It is as if Luke also intends to connect Paul's new identity not so much with his conversion on the Damascus road but rather with the realization of his mission and new commission to evangelize to the Gentiles.

Like many scholars, F. C. Baur bases Luke's shift of Paul's name, not in Acts 13:13, but on Acts 13:9, as his "first important apostolic act,"[122] in the conversion of the Roman proconsul Sergius Paulus. However, a closer examination of the name formula in this verse reveals a variance that seems

---

[121] McRay, 26.

[122] F. C. Baur, *Paul: The Apostle of Jesus Christ* (Grand Rapids, MI: Baker Academic, 2011), 96.

to point to verse 13, and not verse 9, as Luke's target text for Paul's new identity. Before Luke shifts to the exclusive use of the name "Paul" in verse 13, he first refers to Paul as "Saul, who was also called Paul" (v. 9). This is the same formula he uses for Mark (Acts 12:12, 25), and its use here again illustrates Paul's apparent transition from Jewish to Gentile ministries that is not made complete until verse 13. This is not to say that Paul abandoned the Jewish mission and preached exclusively toward the Gentiles at this point. Rather, Luke intends to illustrate that Paul, like Mark, was also experiencing an evolution in his ministry. The unified name of "Paul" symbolizes a man ready to preach to both Jew and Gentile with the zealous objective of creating a community where all the former banners of race, gender, and social status dissipate under the banner of Christ.

Finally, the name order in Acts 13:13 cannot be overlooked, for at this point, Paul is now listed first in order. Luke apparently intends to show that Paul has assumed leadership of the group with a new commission. Thus, three significant textual clues all converge at one single point in Acts 13:13: (1) Luke's use of only "John" to suggest Mark's identity as singularly Hebrew in opposition to Paul's new Gentile agenda; (2) The change in Saul's name to "Paul," to illustrate his new commission to the Gentiles; and (3) the word order of Paul as primary leader of the group. Such narrative precision simply cannot be ignored. With these literary clues in place, we can now examine John Mark's departure with a fresh perspective.

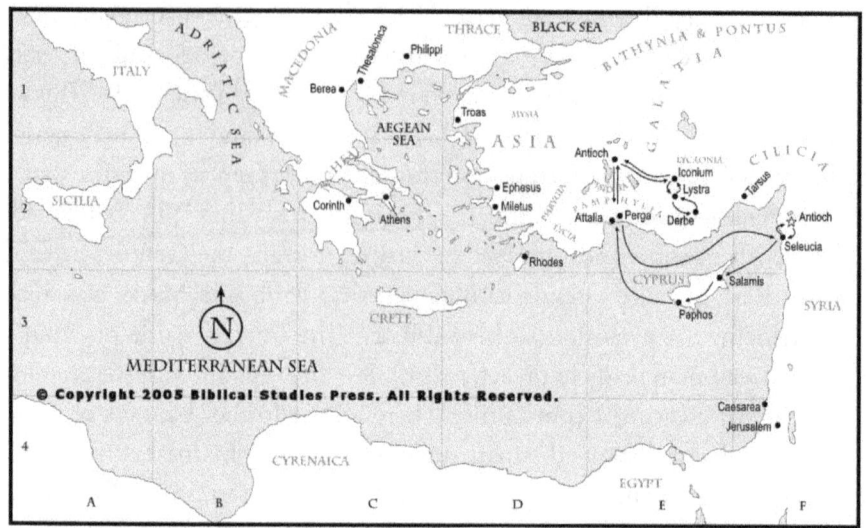

Map courtesy of the NET Bible® http://netbible.com copyright ©1996, 2019
used with permission from Biblical Studies Press, L.L.C. All rights reserved

John Mark Departs from the First Missionary Journey

At the onset, the first Pauline mission was a Jewish mission. Their first stop was the island of Cyprus, Barnabas's home island (Acts 4:36), where at Salamis, "they proclaimed the word of God in the synagogues of the Jews" (13:5). This was most certainly safe and comfortable territory for the missionary bunch, considering that Barnabas was harvesting in his own backyard, and more so in a synagogue where he was raised. In this same verse, Luke inserts another Markan clue, "And they had John to assist them." Initially, this mention may seem as an awkward parenthetical note, but when one compares Mark's behavior in Acts 13:5 with Acts 13:13, the variances are striking. While at Salamis, John Mark readily assists in the evangelism of the Jews in the synagogues, but when they arrive at Perga in Pamphylia, John departs immediately prior to Paul's evangelism of the Gentiles. Worth mention is that Luke records only one conversion during the work on Cyprus. Despite their preaching to the Jews in the synagogues, that one conversion was not even a Jew, but a high-ranking Gentile proconsul—Sergius Paulus. Although the trio may have been encouraged and/or inspired by the work of the Holy Spirit in Sergius

Paulus, the mission work at Cyprus yielded minimal results. It appears that Luke intended to contrast the mostly fruitless work of the Jewish mission at Cyprus with the abundance that was to come by way of the new Gentile mission at Pisidia.

After a brief work on the island of Cyprus, the men continued into the Asian mainland where, from Perga in Pamphylia, John Mark suddenly left them and returned to Jerusalem (Acts 13:13). Although Luke offers no direct explanation for the reasoning behind John Mark's departure, this should not imply that Luke left no textual clues, nor should it imply that his departure was insignificant to the narrative. Assuming the former can lead one to overlook the textual data, while assuming the latter can lead to the assumption that Mark's return "was not disastrous."[123] If Luke's narrative aims to display "the triumph of Christianity in a hostile world,"[124] then one must wonder if Luke intended for that hostility to include the Jewish Christians who opposed the new Gentile mission initiated by Paul and the church at Antioch.

Although cautious circumvention has been a common approach taken toward interpreting this event, a variety of theories have been proffered to explain Mark's sudden departure throughout church history. For example, although Paul later described the dangers he faced while on his missionary journeys (2 Cor. 11:23–28), there is little to support the idea that Mark's departure was due to his unwillingness to be exposed to such perils.[125] The summation of Mark's missionary work, both before and after this event, reveals that he was diligent in the presence of such perils. Other scholars have concluded that Mark's departure was motivated by his disapproval of Paul's assumed leadership, based on Luke's shift in

---

[123] Homer A. Kent, *Jerusalem to Rome: Studies in Acts* (Winona Lake, IN: BMH Books, 1972), 110.

[124] Donald Guthrie, *New Testament Introduction* (Downers Grove, IL: InterVarsity Press, 1970), 353.

[125] Although A. T. Robertson admits John Mark may not have agreed with the change in plans after Paul's assumed leadership and perhaps did not approve of Paul's "aggressive attitude towards the heathen," he concludes that Mark's unwillingness to be exposed to perils was his main motivation for departure based on 2 Cor. 11:26. *The Acts of the Apostles*, Word Pictures in the New Testament, vol. III (Nashville, TN: Broadman Press, 1930), 185.

name order in Acts 13:13.[126] This theory carries some textual weight, but the fact that Barnabas apparently willingly accepted the change in leadership and remained with the mission weakens the argument. Others suggest that Mark grew homesick and desired to return home to see his mother, but again this theory is based on mere conjecture. For example, equally possible is that Mark was motivated to return to Jerusalem in order to report on Paul's new agenda to the Gentiles, and this view at least carries textual support (Acts 15:1, Gal. 2:12). Still others note that Mark was likely of a wealthy household, since his mother's home was large enough to serve as a center for Christian worship, and suggest that perhaps he was not ready for the arduous travel and difficulties experienced in the journey.[127] However, when one examines Mark's complete life and ministry, including his second mission with Barnabas and later work with both Peter and Paul, Mark consistently appears willing to work for long periods away from Jerusalem, leaving little to support this theory. One theory suggests the departure was because "Mark had not yet escaped from Peter's influence."[128] What would such influence entail? If we can assume that it means a preference for Jewish, versus Gentile, evangelism, then this argument begins to tilt toward the direction of a theological-evangelical rift between Mark and Paul.

William Ramsay[129] suggested that Paul contracted malaria when they arrived at Pamphylia, forcing him to alter his plans and head for higher ground to Antioch, and this change of plans caused Mark to abandon the journey since "the new proposal was a departure from the scheme with which they had been charged."[130] Although Ramsay ascribed Paul's contraction of malaria as his "thorn in the flesh" (2 Cor. 12:7–9), there is little to support the idea that this motivated the group to proceed

---

[126] Bruce, *The Book of Acts,* 251.

[127] Louis Barbieri, *Mark*, Moody Gospel Commentary (Chicago: Moody Press, 1995), 15.

[128] G. Campbell Morgan, *The Acts of the Apostles* (New York: Fleming H. Revell, 1924), 323.

[129] William Ramsey (1851–1939) was a biblical archaeologist and NT scholar who served as professor at Oxford University. His numerous contributions, including *St. Paul: The Traveler and Roman Citizen,* contributed greatly to Pauline research and the studies in the church of Acts.

[130] Ramsay, 85–86.

to Pisidian Antioch after their arrival at Pamphylia.[131] Additionally, it seems unlikely that Luke would leave out such an important detail as the contraction of a disease to explain Mark's departure, especially if it provided a justification for his actions. It seems more likely that Luke knew the reasons for Mark's departure but intentionally withheld them because they would distract from the focus of the narrative. Although Ramsay was referring to a departure from the travel agenda, his reference to "a departure from the scheme with which they had been charged" would resonate more if referring to Paul's evangelical agenda.

Numerous scholars have arrived at a similar conclusion that Mark's departure was based, not so much on external circumstances, but on the theological variances that existed between Mark's doctrinal views and Paul's new Gentile agenda. For example, John McRay[132] has noted that Mark's theology was perhaps closer to Peter, his mentor, than Paul's. Although Barnabas was in charge of the mission to Cyprus, which was more Jewish-oriented, "Mark may have become dissatisfied when Paul took the lead *and projected a dangerous and unplanned extension of their mission among the Gentiles of southern Galatia.*"[133] Indeed, Mark's issue may have had more to do with the "dangerous and unplanned extension of their mission" than with Paul's assumed leadership. R. J. Knowling[134] suggests: "Paul's preaching to the Gentiles may have been too liberal for him."[135] Knowling clearly sees the newly assumed Gentile agenda as the divisive issue, but from a traditional Jewish perspective, what exactly would have appeared as "dangerous" or "liberal" for Mark?

Because of Mark's relationship with Barnabas and because the initial

---

[131] Despite the unsettled claim on the source of Paul's persistent ailment, evidence for a type of eye disease seems more convincing (Acts 9:18; Gal. 4:15, 6:11).

[132] John Robert McRay (1931–2018) was an archaeologist and professor of New Testament at Wheaton College. His archaeological work in the biblical lands have contributed greatly to identifying the journeys of Paul and the accounts of the NT church.

[133] Emphasis added. John McRay, *Paul: His Life and Teaching* (Grand Rapids, MI: Baker Academic, 2004), 119.

[134] Richard C. Knowling (1851–1919) was the chaplain of King's College London, canon of Durham, and professor of divinity at Durham University.

[135] R. J. Knowling, *The Acts of the Apostles*, The Expositor's Greek Testament, vol. 2 (Grand Rapids, MI: William B. Eerdmans, 1983), 289.

site of their journey was in Cyprus (Barnabas's home island), it seems reasonable that Mark's motivation to join the men was based more on his relationship with Barnabas than Paul's. Mark and Barnabas were cousins (Col. 4:10), and this relationship seemed to flow deeper than any allegiances to Paul, for when Mark later intended to make a second journey, it was Barnabas who was "prepared to make allowances for him,"[136] while Paul was not. Mark may also have had different expectations of the missionary journey than what eventually unfolded. Barnabas was a Levite (Acts 4:36), and both he and Mark were deeply influenced by Peter, even to the point of prioritizing their Jewish culture over the Gentile agenda at times (Gal. 2:13). To this point, "It may be that Mark had not yet escaped from Peter's influence, even as Peter had not yet escaped from his own more unworthy self."[137] Thus, when Mark's Jewish background and training at the hands of the Jerusalem apostles is considered, his theology seems at odds with what apparently became Paul's new agenda after their arrival at Pamphylia, and this appears to offer a broader explanation for the events that unfold. McRay suggests that "perhaps in theology Mark was closer to Peter and his mission to the Jews (Gal. 2:7) than he was to Paul's Gentile agenda."[138] Paul's new mission to the Gentiles, thus, may have proven too radical for John Mark, a man who, up to that point, was primarily connected to Peter and largely influenced by the theology of the church in Jerusalem.

Immediately following Mark's parting, Paul and Barnabas begin to preach a liberated gospel message to the Gentiles after the Jews reject the gospel (Acts 13:44–48).[139] This textual clue seems to connect Mark's departure with the new missionary agenda that immediately unfolded at Pisidian Antioch, giving the impression that the events surrounding the former were directly motivated by the anticipation of the latter; nor is it a coincidence that Mark returned to Jerusalem, and not Antioch, the site

---

[136] I. Howard Marshall, *Acts*, Tyndale New Testament Commentaries, vol. 5 (Downers Grove, IL: Inter-varsity Press, 1980), 236.

[137] G. Campbell Morgan, 323.

[138] McRay, 119.

[139] Paul and Barnabas's shift toward the Gentiles at this juncture does not indicate "a permanent decision to approach only Gentiles thereafter." Paul continues to address the Jews and the synagogues but with no reservations toward the Gentiles either (Acts 13:14; 14:1; 17:1, 10, 17; 18:4, 19; 19:8): Ben Witherington III, *New Testament History: A Narrative Account*, (Grand Rapids, MI: Baker Academic, 2001), 230–31.

of their original departure. Richard Longenecker[140] makes a distinctive observation: "Mark may have been concerned about the effect news of a direct Christian mission to Gentiles would have in Jerusalem and on the church there and may have wanted to have no part in it."[141] Perhaps Luke intended to suggest that a personal agenda behind Mark's actions was unfolding, and this plan involved his intention to report to the Jerusalem Church on Paul's activities, thus inciting a debate that would later unravel at Antioch.

Perhaps a theological schism existed between Paul and Mark. Because Mark was a member of the conservative Jewish party, he may not have fully accepted Paul's doctrine of salvation by grace through faith alone, suggesting "a serious doctrinal difference with Paul based upon the fact that he (Mark) was still a devout Jew, and at that time unable to accept the doctrine of faith for salvation."[142] John Stott[143] poses perhaps the most stunning question:

> Did [Mark], as a loyal member of Jerusalem's conservative Jewish church, disagree with Paul's bold policy of Gentile evangelism? Was it even he who, on his return to Jerusalem, provoked the Judaizers into opposing Paul?[144]

The weight of Stott's question is found in its explication of what otherwise would seem to be inexplicable behavior on the part of Mark. Longenecker suggests that the conversion of Sergius Paulus at Cyprus may

---

[140] Richard N. Longenecker is a prominent NT scholar who taught at Wycliffe College in the University of Toronto, and was Distinguished Professor of NT at McMaster Divinity College.

[141] Richard N. Longenecker, *The Acts of the Apostles,* The Expositor's Bible Commentary, vol. 9, Frank E. Gaebelein, ed. (Grand Rapids, MI: Zondervan, 1981), 421.

[142] William S. McBirnie, *The Search for the Twelve Apostles,* rev. ed. (Carol Stream, IL: Tyndale Momentum, 2004), 194.

[143] John R. Stott (1921–2011) was an Anglican priest and NT theologian. He is recognized as a leader of the worldwide evangelical movement and was ranked by *Time* magazine as among the one hundred most influential people in the world in 2005.

[144] John R. W. Stott, *The Message of Acts: The Spirit, the Church & the World,* The Bible Speaks Today, John R. W. Stott, ed. (Downers Grove, IL: Inter-Varsity Press, 1990), 221.

have initiated the discussion of a direct approach to the Gentiles, and that "John Mark's departure was because he disagreed with Paul [and] it was his return to ... Jerusalem that may originally have stirred the "Judaizers" in the church to action."[145] These insights not only explain the immediate circumstances surrounding this episode, but they also best interconnect both the preceding and succeeding events of the narrative.

Although some have challenged the idea that Mark's departure was theologically motivated, noting that it "does not square with the undisputed fact that his Gospel was written primarily for Romans," [146] this view assumes no transformative work of the Spirit throughout the years of Mark's life and ministry. The events described in Acts 13:13 occurred at the onset of Mark's ministry (est. AD 48), while his Gospel was written toward the end of his ministerial career (est. AD 65–70),[147] after years of influence and exposure to the Gentile mission. Could any servant of Christ truly remain unaffected by the gospel work over the span of approximately twenty years? Was Peter not convicted and transformed by his own experiences toward the Gentiles? Did Paul not acknowledge the building up into maturity that the Body of Christ would experience by the equipping of the saints for ministry, in order to reach the fullness of Christ (Eph. 4:11–16)? Indeed, it would appear more shocking to see the absence of a transformed perspective (μετάνοια) within the life of a servant by the work and exposure to the kerygma. Although every theory presents its own challenges, not every theory may equally account for the fullness of the textual evidence.

A Word Study on *Apochōreō*

In Acts 13:13 the reader learns that Mark "left" the mission group and returned to Jerusalem, but what exactly did Luke intend by this expression? Although the general translation of the aorist verb *apochōreō* (ἀποχωρέω)

[145] Longenecker, *The Acts of the Apostles,* 421.

[146] John Pollock, *The Apostle: A Life of Paul* (Colorado Springs, CO: ChariotVictor Publishing, 1985), 75.

[147] R. T. France, *The Gospel of Mark: A Commentary on the Greek Text,* The New International Greek Testament Commentary (Grand Rapids, MI: William B. Eerdmans, 2002), 39.

has been rendered as "left" (ESV, NASB, NIV), or "departed" (KJV, NKJV), the synchronic definition is much more emphatic, meaning "to desert" (Sb. 7835, 14; 3 Macc. 2:33), or even an "intentional withdrawal" (Enoch 14:23, 2 Macc. 4:33).[148] Of the only three NT uses of apochōreō, Luke uses the term twice (Lk. 9:39, Acts 13:13), while Matthew uses it only once (Matt. 7:23). In the other two references (Matt. 7:23, Lk. 9:39) the verb clearly carries a more emphatic meaning. For example, Matthew uses the word to describe Jesus's response to the false followers who will be revealed in the end-times, where He declares, "Depart (ἀποχωρεῖτε) from me!" (Matt. 7:23). Luke uses the term one other time in his Gospel, where a father begs Jesus to heal his son from demonic possession and describes the demonic spirit as unwilling to "depart from," or "leave," (ἀποχωρεῖ) from the boy (Lk. 9:39). Additionally, in the LXX, the sole usage of the verbal form (ἀποχωροῦσιν) is found in Jeremiah 26:5, where the Hebrew parallel (סוג) describes a people who had "turned back," tended to "diverge," were "disloyal," and "withdrew" from the Lord.[149]

A diachronic analysis of apochōreō yields similar results. Aside from its meaning to "go away from" (Ar.*Ach*.456; Pl.*R*.394a), it can also specifically apply to the running away of slaves (*PCair.Zen*.15ᵛ.41), and even the withdrawal or "dissent from opinions" (Gal.15.356, cf. Arr.*Epict*.4.1.53).[150] Josephus applies this verb toward one who would "leave" (Ant. 1.261), "retreat" (Ant. 15.149), "return" (Ant. 20.123), "depart" (Wars 1.24), or even "desert" (Wars 6.229).[151] Philo's single use of the term also fits into this syntactical form, meaning to "go away" or "leave" (Mos. 6.77). Thus, one may conclude that, both synchronically and diachronically, nothing casual or flippant is behind the meaning of apochōreō. Rather, its connotation in Acts 13:13 gives every indication that Mark's departure was deliberately hurtful to the mission. Contrary to the assumption that

---

[148] BDAG, 3ʳᵈ ed., 125.

[149] Isaiah Hoogendyk, David DeSilva, Randall Tan, and Rick Brannan, ed. *The Lexham Analytical Lexicon to the Septuagint*. (Bellingham, WA: Lexham Press, 2012).

[150] H. G. Liddell, R. Scott, H. S. Jones, and R. McKenzie, *A Greek-English Lexicon* (Oxford: Clarendon Press, 1996), 228.

[151] Flavius Josephus, *Josephus: The Complete Works*, William Whiston, trans. (Nashville, TN: Thomas Nelson, 1998).

Luke does not explain why Mark "departed" or "left" the mission, perhaps the word speaks for itself.

The internal evidence also supports the idea that Mark's departure in Acts 13:13 carried negative vibes when later, in Acts 15:38, Paul and Barnabas had a "sharp disagreement," severe enough to cause Paul to consider Mark disqualified for a second journey. This would suggest that, whatever intention Mark had for leaving them at Perga, Paul was disappointed by his decision. Nor did Luke use apochōreō to describe Paul's interpretation of Mark's actions in Acts 13:13 but uses the participle form of the verb ἀφίστημι, meaning a deliberate "withdrawal" and even "desertion."[152] Syntactically, the contrastive conjunction δὲ lends semantic force to the phrase, anticipating the connected phrase as contrasting, or oppositional, to the phrase that precedes it.[153] Luke thus appears to identify a significant break in the flow of the narrative in which John Mark's departure not only interrupted the flow of the mission but actually stood in direct opposition to its purpose.

Sometimes, recognizing a word that is not chosen within a context can be just as vital to biblical criticism as in the word that is selected by its author, especially if the word is known and utilized by its author. This is the case for Acts 13:13 where Luke had, at his disposal, other words that could have painted a different scene behind Mark's actions. For example, the seemingly "gentler" verb, *apotassō* (ἀποτάσσω), describes a "man who makes formal parting from his folks."[154] This term described Jesus's gentler parting from the disciples before they went to Bethsaida (Mark 6:46). Nor was this term foreign to Luke, who used apotassō twice, first to describe the man's request to "bid farewell" to his household before following Jesus (Lk. 9:61), and again in Acts 18:18 to describe how Paul "took leave" (ESV, NASB), or "left" (NIV), the church at Corinth in a noticeably polite manner. By using this term, Luke could have clarified that Mark's departure was not a negative act, but rather a more "formal

---

[152] BDAG, 3rd ed., 157.

[153] Daniel B. Wallace, *Greek Grammar: Beyond the Basics* (Grand Rapids, MI: Zondervan, 1996), 671.

[154] G. Kittel and G. W. Bromiley, eds., "ἀποτάσσω," in *Theological Dictionary of the New Testament*, vol. 8 (Grand Rapids, MI: Eerdmans, 2006), 33.

farewell."[155] It would appear that Luke's choice to use apochōreō in order to describe Mark's departure at Perga was precisely motivated to instill tension, not only in the action of Mark's departure, but in the manner of his departure as well. If this be the case, then Mark's departure served as the rising action leading to the climax of Luke's narrative: the eruption of the Gentile controversy.

Unrest in Jerusalem

Any doubt concerning the unrest looming in Jerusalem over the acceptance of the Gentiles quickly dissipates when one examines the activities of the "circumcision party" in relation to the timeline of Gentile evangelism. This group of fundamental Jews criticized Peter for entering the household of a Gentile and practicing table fellowship with "uncircumcised men" (Acts 11:2–3). Luke makes it plain that the occasion for Barnabas's being sent to Antioch was, in part, because the report came to Jerusalem that some of the leaders at Antioch began to preach to the Gentiles (11:20–22). After Paul and Barnabas returned from their first mission, leaders from Jerusalem traveled to Antioch to teach, "Unless you are circumcised according to the custom of Moses, you cannot be saved" (15:1), causing serious dissension within the church. The offensiveness of this issue lay rooted not so much in its communal aspect but in its soteriological assumption. Here, the men from Jerusalem were not only arguing that uncircumcised Gentile believers could not share in table fellowship, but that uncircumcised Gentile believers could not be saved (15:1). Clearly, for these men, circumcision was a matter of salvation and not just an issue of Christian fellowship. This same group also arose in protest at the Jerusalem Council and stood as the clear contestants to Paul's new missionary agenda to the Gentiles (15:5). In Galatians 2:12, Paul described this same, or similar, group, identified as "men from James," who disrupted the church at Antioch, leading both Peter and Barnabas astray.[156] A looming cloud of unrest was apparently stirring in Jerusalem

---

[155] BDAG, 3rd ed., 123.

[156] Although possibly the "men from James" are not identical to the "circumcision group," it appears that their agendas are similar. For the purpose of this argument,

leading up to the Jerusalem Council, and one can only wonder if Mark's report on Paul's activities while in Asia Minor played a decisive role in the disruption that soon followed. Was Mark a member or at least sympathetic to the doctrinal views of this group? Although no clear indication is given, Mark's background and training under Peter would at least have exposed him to the doctrinal weight of their influence.

Two assumptions must be set aside in regard to the "circumcision party." First, it cannot be assumed that this group was acting entirely independently from the position of the mainstream Jerusalem church. When Paul outlines the dissension that arose from this group's visit to Antioch, he describes them as "men from James" (Gal. 2:12), a hint that James, the half brother of Jesus and leader of the church in Jerusalem, had sent them. Considering James's verdict at the Jerusalem Council, possibly these men were not "representing James with full integrity."[157] However, Paul does appear to indicate that these men were acting as representatives from Jerusalem and that the debate that arose at Antioch could only be resolved in a formal gathering at Jerusalem. Second, one should not assume the "circumcision group" did not possess considerable influence, even outside Jerusalem. Paul acknowledges that even Peter feared these men (2:12) and that Barnabas was apparently intimated by them as well (2:13). Paul's description of Peter's separation from the Gentiles lends support for the argument that the "men from James" needed to be taken seriously. The use of the imperfect tense of the verb "separate" (ἀφώριζεν), describes Peter's withdrawal as gradual and not immediate. This suggests that Peter desired to "avert a break between the Jerusalem church and the community of believers at Antioch, even though Paul interpreted his action as doing just the opposite."[158] Simply put, Peter was likely trying to maintain peace between both groups by separating himself from the Gentiles, yet his actions only stirred up the existing unrest.

Undoubtedly, Paul was hurt by what he viewed as betrayal by the

---

I assume both groups as homogenous, based on their parallel agendas. For more information, see Richard N. Longenecker, *Galatians,* Word Biblical Commentary, vol. 41, Ralph P. Martin, ed. (Dallas, TX: Word Books, 1990), 72–75.

[157] Scot McKnight, *Galatians,* The NIV Application Commentary, Terry Muck, ed. (Grand Rapids, MI: Zondervan, 1995), 104.

[158] Richard N. Longenecker, *Galatians,* 74–75.

brothers closest to him, including Peter, Mark, and Barnabas. Mark had abandoned them at Perga. Peter had acted hypocritically, first offering the hand of fellowship to the Gentiles, only to withdraw when the Jewish representatives from Jerusalem arrived. To make matters worse, even Barnabas, Paul's closest ally, followed Peter's example and withdrew from the Gentiles. The sting of Barnabas's apparent betrayal must have been particularly sharp, considering the long and fruitful ministries they had shared, both at Antioch and on their first mission. Barnabas had been the one to find and recruit Paul at Tarsus and reintroduce him to the apostles at Jerusalem. Both Paul and Barnabas's loyalties ran deep, and their commitment to the Gentile cause had always been in unison. Paul singles out that "even Barnabas was led astray" (Gal. 2:13) because, of all people, "Barnabas should have known better."[159] Although Luke describes Mark as the primary reason for Paul and Barnabas's split after the Jerusalem Council, this unsettling event most likely also played a role in that separation.

If Paul's account of the events that unfolded at Antioch are to be taken at face value, then Peter's and Barnabas's withdrawal from the Gentiles lacked integrity. Since Paul offers no response on the part of Peter, then his rebuke of Peter's behavior was apparently valid and received with humility. As mentioned earlier, it may be that Peter's motivation to withdraw was intended to appease the apparent unrest brewing in Jerusalem. However, because his actions influenced other Jews to follow suit, it only heightened the discord when Paul confronted him publicly. The former Pharisee was not one to shy away from conflict, nor was he apprehensive about Peter's stature in the church. For Paul, "it was not peace at any price, but the gospel at all costs."[160]

Taking Mark's prior departure at Perga into account, it becomes easier to see how Paul would have felt ostracized by those around him. Although scholars debate the eventual outcome of this conflict, the collective decision later reached at Jerusalem clearly went in favor of Paul's view. It seems much more likely that Peter accepted Paul's rebuke, because it is highly unlikely that Paul would have even mentioned this incident if the confrontation

---

[159] Craig Keener, *Galatians*, 160.
[160] Philip G. Ryken, *Galatians,* Reformed Expository Commentary, Daniel M. Doriani, ed. (Phillipsburg, NJ: P&R Publishing, 2005), 57.

had ended in failure. Additionally, Peter's public support of Paul's new Gentile mission at the Jerusalem Council demonstrates that Paul's rebuke was indeed received with a humble heart.

Where does one place the events surrounding Paul's encounter with Peter at Antioch (Gal. 2:11–14), in relation to Luke's chronology in Acts? This is particularly important for Mark's timeline, assuming Peter continued to hold an influence over his young disciple. Two key events must be considered in relation to the events outlined in Galatians: (1) The Cornelius event and (2) the Jerusalem Council. A case can be made for these events occurring either before or after the controversy at Antioch. However, only one sequence seems best to align with both Luke's and Paul's accounts.

1. The Cornelius event—In the Cornelius narrative (Acts 10), Peter experiences two events that seem to overturn his prior attitude toward the Gentiles. First, his vision at Joppa reveals to him that the Gentiles are now qualified to share in table fellowship. After he preaches to Cornelius and his household, he witnesses the power of the Holy Spirit come upon the Gentiles through the miracle of glossolalia, which reveals to Peter that the Gentiles are now eligible to join the Christian church apart from circumcision. By Peter's own testimony, he tells Cornelius that up until that time he had not associated with Gentiles nor shared in table fellowship (Acts 10:28). Therefore, if the events at Antioch had occurred prior to the Cornelius event, it would contradict Peter's own testimony, since Peter was already practicing table fellowship at Antioch prior to the controversy. Admittedly, it is feasible that Peter was practicing table fellowship with circumcised Gentiles at Antioch and that the Cornelius event preceded the controversy outlined in Galatians. However, Peter tells Cornelius and those with him that it was forbidden for a Jew to even "*associate with* … anyone of another nation" (10:28) and makes no reference to circumcision. Additionally, Peter uses the term *allophylos* (ἀλλόφυλος) to mean "alien," "foreigner," or, from the Judean viewpoint, as "outsider" or

"gentile."[161] Since Cornelius was already a "God-fearer" (10:2),[162] Peter is likely speaking of his unprecedented move of associating with a person of another nation, regardless of circumcision. It thus seems best to view Peter's encounter with Cornelius as preceding the events outlined by Paul in Galatians, since "association" was exactly what Peter was doing at Antioch. Of course, this would mean that Peter's actions appeared hypocritical and in direct contradiction to what he reported earlier to the Jerusalem Church concerning Cornelius (11:1–18), and that is exactly the point behind Paul's rebuke. This also coincides with Luke's chronology, since he places Peter's account prior to Paul and Barnabas's return from their first missionary journey. This would keep Luke's chronology intact and place the Cornelius event as occurring prior to both his visit to Antioch and the convening of the Jerusalem Council.

2. The Jerusalem Council—The Jerusalem Council (Acts 15) is a key event in relation to the controversy at Antioch (Gal. 2:11–14). At the Jerusalem Council, Peter publicly supported Paul's Gentile mission, in apparent contrast to his actions at Antioch. If the events at Antioch occurred after the convening of the Jerusalem Council, then it describes Peter as dishonest and fickle, having initially offered his public support for Paul and Barnabas at Jerusalem, only to retract it later at Antioch. Although Peter displayed such weakness prior to the resurrection event (Matt. 26:69–75), we see no such behavior with the recommissioned Peter, who boldly preached the gospel at Pentecost. So also, the behavior of the "men from James" would at best appear hypocritical and at worst appear mutinous, if this event had occurred after James's endorsement of open table fellowship at the Jerusalem Council. More importantly, if the verdict at the council had already been given, Paul would have been quick to reference it in his confrontation with Peter, yet no such mention is given. As such, the events at Antioch resonate that a consensus had yet to be reached. It is important to note that the disagreement between Paul and Peter was not theological, because Peter was already eating with Gentiles when the representatives

---

[161] BDAG, 3rd ed., 48.

[162] See subchapter "Greeks, Proselytes, and 'God-Fearers'" under chapter 1.

from Jerusalem arrived, demonstrating that Peter had already accepted Gentile fellowship. Therefore, the real issue was "over behavior, not over the content of the gospel message."[163] Paul's account describes Peter as timid and hypocritical, unable to put into practice what he already knew was an acceptable practice in the church—table fellowship with uncircumcised Gentiles. This description precisely parallels Paul's criticism of Peter's actions in Galatians. If the Jerusalem Council had yet to convene, then how would Peter know? The answer is the Cornelius event, which had transpired prior to his visit to Antioch. Also likely is that Luke cited the controversy at Antioch, outlined in Galatians 2:11–14, in the events described in Acts 15:2, leading immediately up to the Jerusalem Council. If the events outlined in Galatians occurred prior to the Jerusalem Council, this would then place Paul's visit described in Galatians 2:1 as his second visit, likely his "famine visit," prior to his third visit to the Jerusalem Council.[164] Thus, it seems best to fit the Jerusalem Council as immediately succeeding the controversy that arose at Antioch, but preceding the Cornelius event.

With Peter's timeline in place, we now have a chronology that can link both Luke's and Paul's accounts, and that can shed greater light on Mark's activities. But how does Peter's chronology help us better understand Mark's narrative? Putting the chronological pieces together, as described above, one obtains a clearer picture of what happened to Mark after his departure from Perga. After hearing of Paul's new Gentile agenda, Mark boards a ship back to Jerusalem with the intention of reporting on Paul's activities. However, upon his return to Jerusalem, Mark discovers the church had shifted in its views on Gentile fellowship while he had been ministering at Antioch with Paul and Barnabas. He hears the amazing story of what happened to Peter, both at Joppa and Caesarea. His mentor's vision at Joppa, making what was once unclean now clean, shakes Mark to the core. He is shocked to hear Peter's account of how the miracle of tongues, which had occurred at Pentecost for the Jews, was now duplicated over

---

[163] Keener, *Galatians*, 158.
[164] Longenecker, *Galatians*, 46.

the Gentiles at Caesarea (Acts 10:44–46). Mark then begins to rethink his prior convictions. If the Holy Spirit had revealed such marvels to his spiritual mentor, had he been wrong to abandon the mission at Perga?

However, Mark's report to the leaders of the Jerusalem church about Paul's new approach to Gentile evangelism is still received with great concern by an influential group … the "circumcision group." A small assembly, described by Paul as the "men from James" (Gal. 2:12), is gathered and awaits news of Paul and Barnabas's return in order to head to Antioch and address the issue. When Paul and Barnabas return from their first incursion into Asia, they report on their great success, and the church rejoices. Peter arrives and rejoices with them in communion and table fellowship (2:11), but when the "men from James" hear of Paul's return, they immediately head to Antioch, and the grumbling soon begins. Upon their arrival, Peter retracts from the Gentiles, and Barnabas immediately follows suit. Paul publicly confronts the existing hypocrisy, and a great debate unfolds (Acts 15:2). The dissension results in the group agreeing to take the matter to Jerusalem, and a council is formed with respective representatives elected from both sides of the debate. Through it all, Mark is behind the scenes, watching God's plan of salvation to the Gentiles slowly unfold.

Whether Mark traveled back to Antioch and witnessed the controversy between Peter and Paul unfold firsthand or whether he remained at Jerusalem and heard the reports of the events leading up to the Jerusalem Council is irrelevant. What matters is that Mark now faced a new decision concerning the Gentiles. Although Paul was hurt by what Mark had done to them on the first mission, what he did not yet know was that the Holy Spirit would use the unrest in Jerusalem to incite a renewed conviction in Mark, and indeed everyone in attendance. It would soon become evident that the invitation to the Gentiles was not a deviation from God's plan of salvation but rather was the ancient and divine promise that was now ready to be fulfilled.

CHAPTER 4

THE GENTILE PROMISE IS FULFILLED

𝒲hen the Christian movement began, before long Jewish believers recognized that the former practices used to induct Gentiles into the fold of their synagogues (i.e., submission to the Mosaic custom of circumcision and observance of the Torah), could no longer work within the theological confines of Christianity. Jesus had changed everything. The sacrificial death and resurrection of Jesus Christ had now revealed the true basis for the salvation of humankind (Rom. 1:1–5). Simply put, faith in Jesus and not ritualistic observation of the Mosaic Law brought about true salvation for both Jew and Gentile alike (Gal. 3:10–14). Thus, to continue to insist upon Gentile submission to the Torah was paramount to contradicting the theological meaning and purpose behind Christ's death. Before Christ, the Mosaic Law had functioned as the "guardian" (παιδαγωγός) over righteousness (Gal. 3:24), and so it made sense for the Jews to bring the Gentiles into the fold by means of the Torah. But now, a new day had come in which the righteousness of Christ was now available to all by grace through faith (Eph. 2:8). This demanded a reprioritization of the Mosaic Law, not to discard it entirely, but to set it in its proper place as the national and ethnic identifier of Israel's history and not as the ways and means of salvation.

Paul not only understood this radical shift brought about by Christ's resurrection, he championed its cause within the emerging Christian church. The man once regarded as the "Hebrew of Hebrews" (Phil. 3:5), made it clear that circumcision no longer mattered, and any who insisted upon Gentile submission to this tradition rejected the true call of God ...

Only let each person lead the life that the Lord has assigned to him, and to which God has called him. This is my rule in all the churches. Was anyone at the time of his call already circumcised? Let him not seek to remove the marks of circumcision. Was anyone at the time of his call uncircumcised? Let him not seek circumcision. For neither circumcision counts for anything nor uncircumcision but keeping the commandments of God. Each one should remain in the condition in which he was called (1 Cor. 7:17–20).

It is incorrect to say that Paul believed the Mosaic Law no longer produced righteousness in an individual. On the contrary, Paul argued that it never could (Gal. 2:16)! Nor did Paul believe that righteous behavior was not foundational to the life of the Christian, for he was convinced that the new "walk" (περιπατέω) in Christ moved, beyond merely a new attitude or perspective, to an effective life in which their "habit of conduct"[165] produced good works (Eph. 2:10). What the shift from Torah to a Christ-based faith did mean was that the harvest fields of the earth were now unfenced and unobstructed (Lk. 10:2–3). Paul was convinced that now was the time to take the full and unimpeded power of the gospel to the Gentiles. Paul's revelation was both magnificent and bold, but it was also dangerous. Not all Jewish Christians would be so ready and willing to overturn generations of spiritual traditions in order to embrace Paul's new revelation. This challenge was at the nucleus of the Gentile issue, and it appears that Luke intended for its eruption to revolve around Mark's departure at Perga at Pamphylia.

The conversion of the Roman proconsul, Sergius Paulus (Acts 13:12), may have had a direct impact upon Paul's decision to initiate his new missionary agenda. It is striking that Luke notes Sergius Paulus's conversion in the verse immediately preceding John Mark's departure. It may be that Paul used this Gentile conversion as an apologetic basis in which to reveal his new missionary plan to Barnabas and Mark on their way to the Asian mainland. Because Mark chose to return to Jerusalem and not to Antioch, he may have intended to report on Paul's new Gentile agenda and perhaps

---

[165] Walter Bauer, "περιπατέω," BDAG, 3rd ed.

garner advocates for his position. Ben Witherington[166] also leaves open the possibility that Mark's return to Jerusalem, and not to Antioch, was for the purpose of "reporting on this new venture."[167] Perhaps his report motivated the specific group of Jews mentioned in Acts 15:1 to make their way to Antioch to challenge Paul's theology (and authority), which stirred the Gentile controversy into motion.

After Mark's departure, Paul and Barnabas headed for Pisidian Antioch, where they once again began to preach at the synagogue. But this time, because of the Jews' rejection of their preaching, Paul and Barnabas declared that they would now offer the gospel freely to the Gentiles (Acts 13:46). That Paul or Barnabas understood the significance of this event is hard to imagine. Here and now, the promise uttered by God to Abraham long ago was now being fulfilled! When the Lord called Abraham to leave his home and go to a new land, He did so with a promise and a blessing, "I will bless those who bless you, and him who dishonors you I will curse, *and in you all the families of the earth shall be blessed*" (Gen. 12:3). Abraham's faith established him as the father to the nation of Israel, but he never ceased being the father to all the families of the earth. Paul understood that Jesus had now become Abraham's promised heir (Gal. 3:29). By His death and resurrection, God's long-awaited promise to bless all earthly families was now being realized. On that fateful day on the dusty streets of Pisidian Antioch, Paul and Barnabas ushered in the age of the Gentiles.

Paul Responds to the Judaizers

If we need any indication of the offensiveness of Paul's new plan to the Gentiles, we need look no further than in the account of his stoning at Lystra, where Luke notes that "Jews came from Antioch and Iconium" (Acts 14:19), to stir up the crowd and incite them to stone Paul. Because Antioch and Iconium were the two preceding cities Paul and Barnabas

---

[166] Ben Witherington III is Amos Professor of NT for Doctoral Studies at Asbury Theological Seminary in Wilmore, Kentucky, and is on the doctoral faculty at St. Andrews University in Scotland. Dr. Witherington is considered one of today's foremost scholars in NT studies.

[167] Witherington III, 404.

had visited prior to their arrival at Lystra, this group of Jews had followed Paul and Barnabas to Lystra with the direct intention of warning the other Jewish communities about Paul's message.[168] Iconium was approximately twenty miles away from Lystra, and Pisidian Antioch was approximately a hundred miles away, about a four or five-day journey.[169] Imagine what great offense and emotional discord Paul's preaching was producing in these two cities that motivated the Jews to travel this distance in order to oppose Paul's mission! Word traveled fast, and it was only a matter of time before the news of Paul's activities would reach the doors of the Jerusalem church. The question is, who would deliver it?

When Paul and Barnabas returned to Antioch from their first mission, they gathered the church together and reported on how God "had opened a door of faith to the Gentiles" (Gal. 14:27). One can sense the spiritual excitement flowing through the congregation as they rejoiced over the success of Paul and Barnabas's mission! However, just as rapidly as the spirits were lifted at Antioch over their reports, Luke immediately dampens the mood with the arrival of the Judean representatives:

> But some men came down from Judea and were teaching the brothers, "Unless you are circumcised according to the custom of Moses, you cannot be saved" (Acts 15:1).[170]

Luke notes that "no small dissension" resulted between Paul and Barnabas, and the men from Judea, as the men debated the issue. Luke's use of the Greek terms *stasis* and *zētēsis* illustrates that the issue had now

---

[168] Keener, *Acts,* 2175.

[169] Ibid.

[170] Luke begins this transitional statement with the common conjunction καί. This term can take on different meanings depending on context, including "even," "and," "also," and "but." The question is, which meaning did Luke intend for this conjunction? Although various translations choose to omit this conjunction altogether (NIV, NASB, HCSB, NLT), other translations have opted to apply it either as the connective conjunction "and" (KJV, NKJV), or as the contrastive conjunction "but" (ESV, RSV). Considering the adversative context of the pericope, the contrastive use of "but" seems most fitting. See Daniel B. Wallace, *Greek Grammar: Beyond the Basics: An Exegetical Syntax of the New Testament* (Grand Rapids, MI: Zondervan, 1996), 671.

become "volatile."[171] We are not certain if Mark had returned to Antioch with this group of men from Judea but more likely is that he remained in Jerusalem after his return and was in attendance at the Jerusalem Council. If the men from Judea were convicted to go to Antioch because of Mark's report on Paul's activities, Paul likely would have connected the dots and surmised that Mark's betrayal at Perga had followed him to Jerusalem. It was time for Paul to respond to the "Judaizers," and respond he did! Although space eludes us for a more extensive analysis of Paul's *apologia* against the "circumcision group,"[172] at least a brief analysis is warranted in order to better understand the theological climate surrounding the Jerusalem Council.

One of the Pauline defenses against the "Judaizers" that is not commonly referenced today is found in Galatians 3:19–29. Paul's letter to the Galatians is unique for two reasons. First, in contrast to Paul's other letters, Galatia was not a city, but a region. Where we might quickly connect Paul's other letters to their respective cities (Thessalonica to Thessalonians, Ephesus to Ephesians, Philippi to Philippians, Rome to Romans, etc.),[173] the letter to the Galatians is addressed to the assemblage of churches Paul established in the region of Galatia (Gal. 1:2).[174] If Paul intended this letter to make its way through the churches of Galatia, then it means that, not long after he established these embryonic Christian missions, Jewish conservatives were already at work pressing its Gentile members to

---

[171] *A Bible Handbook to the Acts of the Apostles,* Mal Couch, ed. (Grand Rapids, MI: Kregel Publications, 1999), 318.

[172] Indeed, the Pauline literature is immersed in the Gentile matter, and a plethora of resources exist that address Paul's works on this topic. For a more thorough analysis of Paul's debate surrounding the Jerusalem Council, see the most excellent analysis by Craig S. Keener, *Galatians: A Commentary* (Grand Rapids, MI: Baker Academic, 2019), 6–45.

[173] Although some of these letters may indeed have been intended to be read beyond their immediate churches and used as circulatory letters, the fact that they were addressed to a particular church within a particular city is the point argued here.

[174] Proponents of the Southern Galatian view commonly connect the churches of Pisidian Antioch, Iconium, Lystra, and Derbe, the churches Paul established on his first missionary journey, as the intended recipients of Paul's letter to the Galatians. That is the view presupposed here. For broader discussion on the North-South Galatian hypotheses, see Craig S. Keener, *Galatians* (Grand Rapids, MI: Baker Academic, 2019), 16–22.

submit to circumcision. Second, Galatians may indeed be the first of Paul's epistles, and possibly even written after the close of his first missionary journey and even prior to the Jerusalem Council.[175] If indeed "it might be possible to date Galatians before the Jerusalem Council of Acts 15:6ff,"[176] then this letter stands as the unique text most closely written to the events surrounding John Mark's departure and the Jewish-Gentile controversy preceding the convening of the Jerusalem Council. Indeed, one can almost hear these words proclaimed from the lips of Paul during the dissension that broke out at Antioch (Acts 15:2)! The churches in Galatia (as well as Antioch), were being pressured by a group of conservative Jews to submit the Gentiles to circumcision in order to be considered "true children of Abraham (Gal. 3:7). Paul responds with a heavy reliance on the OT, second only to Romans in proportionate use with at least ten formal citations in six chapters,[177] in order to prove to his Jewish opponents that his evangelism to the Gentiles was not only permissible, but actually providential, based on God's preordained promise of salvation.

Although some scholars view Paul's excursus in Galatians 3:19–29 as a "digression on the Torah" that contains a series of "very concise and unconnected statements,"[178] one would err to view this passage as incidental. For in this section, "Paul comes to the heart of his differences with the Judaizers,"[179] by arguing that submission to the Torah had now been replaced by faith in Jesus Christ as the agency of salvation. This idea stood in stark contrast to traditional Judaism and the belief that the Torah was the eternal form of obtaining righteousness with God. In verse 19, Paul begins with an indefinite temporal clause, "until the offspring should come" (ἄχρις οὗ ἔλθῃ τὸ σπέρμα), arguing that the true purpose of the

---

[175] Ronald Y. K. Fung, *The Epistle to the Galatians*, The New International Commentary on the New Testament, Gordon Fee, ed. (Grand Rapids, MI: William B. Eerdmans, 1988), 9.

[176] Bruce, *Galatians*, 44.

[177] Moises Silva, "Galatians," in *Commentary on the New Testament Use of the Old Testament*, G. K. Beale and D. A. Carson (Grand Rapids, MI: Baker Academic, 2007), 785. http://ebookcentral.proquest.com/lib/liberty/detail. action?docID=3117030.

[178] Hans D. Betz, *Galatians*, Hermeneia–A Critical and Historical Commentary on the Bible (Philadelphia: Fortress Press), 63.

[179] Longenecker, *Galatians,* 136.

submit to circumcision. Second, Galatians may indeed be the first of Paul's epistles, and possibly even written after the close of his first missionary journey and even prior to the Jerusalem Council.[175] If indeed "it might be possible to date Galatians before the Jerusalem Council of Acts 15:6ff,"[176] then this letter stands as the unique text most closely written to the events surrounding John Mark's departure and the Jewish-Gentile controversy preceding the convening of the Jerusalem Council. Indeed, one can almost hear these words proclaimed from the lips of Paul during the dissension that broke out at Antioch (Acts 15:2)! The churches in Galatia (as well as Antioch), were being pressured by a group of conservative Jews to submit the Gentiles to circumcision in order to be considered "true children of Abraham (Gal. 3:7). Paul responds with a heavy reliance on the OT, second only to Romans in proportionate use with at least ten formal citations in six chapters,[177] in order to prove to his Jewish opponents that his evangelism to the Gentiles was not only permissible, but actually providential, based on God's preordained promise of salvation.

Although some scholars view Paul's excursus in Galatians 3:19–29 as a "digression on the Torah" that contains a series of "very concise and unconnected statements,"[178] one would err to view this passage as incidental. For in this section, "Paul comes to the heart of his differences with the Judaizers,"[179] by arguing that submission to the Torah had now been replaced by faith in Jesus Christ as the agency of salvation. This idea stood in stark contrast to traditional Judaism and the belief that the Torah was the eternal form of obtaining righteousness with God. In verse 19, Paul begins with an indefinite temporal clause, "until the offspring should come" (ἄχρις οὗ ἔλθη τὸ σπέρμα), arguing that the true purpose of the

---

[175] Ronald Y. K. Fung, *The Epistle to the Galatians*, The New International Commentary on the New Testament, Gordon Fee, ed. (Grand Rapids, MI: William B. Eerdmans, 1988), 9.

[176] Bruce, *Galatians,* 44.

[177] Moises Silva, "Galatians," in *Commentary on the New Testament Use of the Old Testament*, G. K. Beale and D. A. Carson, ed. (Grand Rapids, MI: Baker Academic, 2007), 785. http://ebookcentral.proquest.com/lib/liberty/detail.action?docID=3117030.

[178] Hans D. Betz, *Galatians*, Hermeneia—A Critical and Historical Commentary on the Bible (Philadelphia: Fortress Press, 1979), 163.

[179] Longenecker, *Galatians,* 136.

law actually increased "the sum-total of transgression."[180] Simply put, he argued that the Mosaic Law had not improved the plight of humanity. It had only made things worse by revealing the true width and breadth of humanity's sin.

Paul's declaration in verse 20 that "God is one" has produced numerous interpretations. However, the solution may be found in his later statement that all are "one in Christ Jesus" (v. 28). This may indicate that Moses, the mediator of the Mosaic Law, represented a division of parties, while Christ has united all as one party. Paul argues that "any transaction in which a mediator is involved is inferior to one in which God acts directly."[181] Moses had served as the temporal, and imperfect, mediator between Israel and God, but only Jesus could now serve directly on our behalf. From a temporal view, the implication is clear—where once we were divided by the Law, we are now made as one in Christ. Paul's argument here does not stand in contrast to Judaic thought, for his argument echoed the *Shema*, that "God is one" (Deut. 6:4) and would have served to remind his opposition of God's original eschatological plan of salvation.

In verse 21, Paul clarifies that, although the Law does not stand in contrast to the promises of God,[182] it is incapable of providing what the Judaizers had always claimed it could do—give life. Here, he argues against the common Rabbinic teaching that the one who follows the Law "will find life by them" (Sir. 17:11, '*Abot* 2.8).[183] However, this does not imply that the Law stands in contrast to God. Paul's voluntative optative expression, "Certainly not!" or "May it never be!" (μὴ γένοιτο) at the beginning of the verse emphatically denies such implications. Rather, Paul offers a second-class conditional statement, "For if a law had been given," in which the protasis describes the limitations of the Law's ability to impart life by the complementary adverbial infinitive phrase, "that could give

---

[180] Bruce, *Galatians*, 175.

[181] H. D. Betz, 171–73.

[182] Although the words τοῦ Θεοῦ are absent from several early manuscripts (𝔓⁴⁶, B, Ambrosiaster Marius Victorinus), this may also be due to "an accident in transmission" and are enclosed within brackets. Bruce M. Metzger, *A Textual Commentary on the Greek New Testament*, 2nd ed. (Deutsche Bibelgesellschaft, 2016), 526.

[183] Douglas J. Moo, *Galatians*, Baker Exegetical Commentary on the New Testament, Robert W. Yarbrough and Robert H. Stein, eds. (Grand Rapids, MI: Baker Academic, 2013), 239.

life" (ὁ δυνάμενος ζῳοποιῆσαι), and then seals its dysfunction through the apodosis, "then righteousness would indeed be by the law" (ἂν ἦν ἡ δικαιοσύνη). It is as if Paul is asking, if the Law was truly intended to make us righteous, then why are we not righteous?

In verse 22, Paul contends that the source of true life is found not in the Torah but in Jesus Christ. Whether the genitive construction, ἐκ πίστεως Ἰησοῦ Χριστοῦ, should be viewed objectively (faith in Christ) or subjectively (faithfulness of Christ) within the aspect of Paul's temporal argument, the point is that Jesus Christ, and not the Law, serves as the true source of salvation history. Thus, Paul argues that the Law was not only temporal but temporal with an intentional purpose—to lead us to Christ. In verse 23, Paul again illustrates the temporal nature of the Law, as indicated by the dual temporal clauses: "before faith came ... until the coming faith would be revealed." Here, Paul means to show that the Law was only temporary, serving to keep God's people in temporary custody, using the imperfect form of the passive verb "imprisoned" or "detained," (φρουρέω). This custody has been kept "under the law," with the express purpose of waiting "before faith came." The inferential appositional phrase in verse 24, "So then, the law" (ὥστε ὁ νόμος), reveals the identity of the "guardian" (παιδαγωγός) as the indirect object of "became" (γέγονεν), with "until Christ" (εἰς Χριστόν) as the genitive of destination, and "by faith" (ἐκ πίστεως) as the genitive of means. Simply put, Paul is saying that the Law could never do what the Judaizers were claiming it could do. Its true purpose was to guard us, prepare us, with the sole purpose of leading us to Christ.

Paul's argument on the temporality of the Law comes to a climax in verses 25–29, where he argues that because faith has now arrived, those formerly under the Law are now sons of God by the *agency*, "in Christ Jesus" (ἐν Χριστῷ Ἰησοῦ), and the *means,* "through faith" (διὰ τῆς πίστεως). The phrase "in Christ" is a Pauline favorite meant "to signal the personal, local, and dynamic relation of the believer to Christ."[184] Now, there is no longer "Jew nor Greek, there is neither slave nor free, there is no male and female, for you are all one in Christ Jesus" (Gal. 3:28). These words would serve as a challenge for the traditional Jews, including the Judaizers, to determine where their allegiance truly stood—in Torah or Christ? Paul concludes his

---

[184] Longenecker, *Galatians,* 152.

argument with a first-class conditional statement in which the "offspring" (σπέρμα) are now identified with the protasis: "And if you are Christ's" (εἰ δὲ ὑμεῖς Χριστοῦ). As true descendants of Abraham made possible by the agency of Christ, they are now the promised heirs. Paul's argument for the true children of Abraham in this passage was most likely a response to the view of the Mishnah that considered even the full Gentile proselyte as unqualified to call Abraham "father."[185]

Within the structure of Galatians 3:19–29, four identifiable temporal clauses are also evident that help frame Paul's description of the Mosaic Law's temporal elements. The first is found in verse 19, where Paul explains that the Law was ordained "until the seed would come." Here, the subjunctive indefinite temporal clause "indicates a future contingency,"[186] illustrating that although the Mosaic Law was temporal, it was also intentionally leading God's people to an eventual fulfillment in Christ. The preposition "until" (ἄχρις) serves as a clear "marker of continuous extent of time up to a point,"[187] with the "offspring" (σπέρμα) serving as the connective point between the anticipated event in verse 19, and its arrival in verse 25. The second and third temporal clauses are found in verse 23, in which Paul speaks "in a pointedly temporal fashion,"[188] by noting that the Law performed its function as a "custodian" until faith arrived, describing a new phase of God's salvation history. Paul uses the "guardian" (παιδαγωγός) as an intentional metaphor aimed at demonstrating the temporal function of the Law, in the same way that a custodian, or tutor, in Roman times would care for an adolescent only until he reached late adolescence.[189] Again, Paul aims to reveal that the Law did its duty, but only until faith would come—that is, faith in Jesus Christ. Within this context, εἰς is translated temporally ("until"), a notably rare use of this preposition in Pauline style.[190] The fourth, and final, temporal clause is found in verse

---

[185] Stein, 337.

[186] Wallace, 479.

[187] BDAG, 3rd ed., 160.

[188] Benjamin Schliesser, "'Christ-Faith' as an Eschatological Event (Galatians 3:23–26): A 'Third View' on Πίστις Χριστοῦ," *Journal for the Study of the New Testament*, 38, no. 3 (2016): 283. sagepub.co.uk/journalsPermissions.nav.

[189] Timothy George, *Galatians*, The New American Commentary, vol. 30, E. Ray Clendenen, ed. (Nashville, TN: B&H Publishing, 1994), 265.

[190] Keener, *Galatians,* 289n.

25, the concluding verse. Here, Paul resolves the anticipation initially set forth in verse 19, by announcing that, indeed, faith has now arrived. The promised seed, identified as "faith" (πίστις), is Christ himself, and His arrival has revealed the temporal elements of the Law and now ushered in "the era of faith."[191] What does Paul intend to illustrate through these four temporal clauses? Simply that the Law was never intended to serve as the permanent solution for this world. Christ was God's permanent solution to the condition of fallen humanity.

Until his encounter with Christ, Paul would have undoubtedly held a similarly eternal view of the Torah, but his theology had been radically tested through his encounter with Christ. Paul now viewed the Mosaic Law as functioning within a temporal epoch until the coming of Christ, and this view would have undoubtedly deviated widely from that of traditional Judaism.[192] What Paul argued in Galatians 3:19–29 would have seemed astonishing to the Jews who heard it, for traditional Judaism held the Torah as "the law that endures forever" (Bar 4:1).[193] It seems apparent that this was the basis for the Judaizers' insistence that the Galatians adopt the covenant of circumcision and subscribe to the Torah (and the reason for my election and analysis of these verses). Paul countered by insisting that the Torah should serve only "up to the time that people could put their trust in Jesus Christ."[194] Paul did not merely insist on the Law as temporal, as a type of isolated event in history, but rather placed it in its proper relation to the progress of salvation history.[195] The brilliance behind Paul's new theology lay not only in its ceasing to be a necessity for Gentiles but also in its redefining of what it meant to be a Jew. Paul challenged his opponents' "ethnic memory" by prioritizing the Abrahamic promise over the Mosaic Law, demonstrating that the true children of Abraham were those who identified themselves not by observance of the Torah but by

---

[191] Scot McKnight, *Galatians*, The NIV Application Commentary, Terry Muck, ed. (Grand Rapids, MI: Zondervan, 1995), 182.

[192] Longenecker, *Galatians* 139.

[193] Thomas R. Schreiner, *Galatians*, Exegetical Commentary on the New Testament, Clinton E. Arnold, ed. (Grand Rapids, MI: Zondervan, 2010), 241.

[194] Daniel C. Arichea Jr. and Eugene A. Nida, *A Translator's Handbook on Paul's Letter to the Galatians* (New York: United Bible Societies, 1976), 80.

[195] Fung, 169.

faith in Christ.[196] The question now remained, could Jewish and Gentile Christians sit at the table of fellowship in unison and coexist as true children of Abraham?

The Jerusalem Council

It was at Jerusalem where the central Jewish concern arose: "Unless you are circumcised according to the custom of Moses, you cannot be saved" (Acts 15:1). This verse forms a major chronological juncture in Luke's narrative, for although the first fourteen chapters only offer glimpses of the emerging Jewish-Gentile controversy, primarily in the Cornelius event, at this point the Gentile issue comes to the forefront and forms the structural and theological center of Acts.[197] Although there were clearly Christian Jews that held to the requirements of the Mosaic Law for Gentiles (11:2, 15:1), Peter's report of his vision at Joppa (10:9–16), his preaching to Cornelius (10:34–43), and the resulting Jewish witness of glossolalia that befell the Gentiles (10:44–48) may have left the Jerusalem church, and the circumcision group that challenged him, more sympathetic to the Gentile cause. This would also explain why the leaders at Jerusalem decided in favor of Paul's new vision for the Gentiles (15:13–21). From a global perspective, Luke appears to be noting key events in his narrative, leading up to the Jerusalem Council, in which the Holy Spirit was preparing the church to embrace the new Gentile vision.

In the events leading up to the Jerusalem Council, Luke seemed to sketch Peter not as a member of the "circumcision group" but as holding "a mediating position in the confrontation which was gradually shaping up."[198] Although at first Peter seemed reluctant to accept God's vision of open Gentile table fellowship (Acts 10:9–16), he openly submitted to the Spirit's instruction to witness to Cornelius (10:28–29) and interpreted the glossolalia event as the newfound eligibility of Gentiles to be baptized

---

[196] Philip F. Esler, "Paul's Contestation of Israel's (Ethnic) Memory of Abraham in Galatians 3," *Biblical Theology Bulletin* 36, no. 1 (Spring 2006): 23–34, http://link.galegroup.com.ezproxy.liberty.edu/apps/doc/A142569511/AONE?u=vic_liberty&sid=AONE&xid=33278689.

[197] Marshall, 256–57.

[198] Hengel, 92.

free from the Torah (10:44–48). Luke then transitions to the first journey undertaken by Paul, Barnabas, and Mark, seemingly highlighting two points: John Mark's departure and Paul's new missionary agenda to the Gentiles. Luke masterfully uses these narrative blocks in order to build up to the climactic event that takes place in Jerusalem.

As the leaders convened the first order of business at the Jerusalem Council, tensions were likely high, and indecision was in their midst. Which faction would be endorsed? Whose voice would win the day? The meeting began with a report given by Paul and Barnabas on their evangelism ministry to the Gentiles (Acts 15:4). The results had been overwhelmingly successful, and the fruit of the Spirit was evident. Immediately, a group of Christian Jews, described as "the party of the Pharisees,"[199] responded by insisting on circumcision for the Gentiles in order "to keep the law of Moses" (15:5). Interestingly, after some debate, Peter, and not Paul, emerged as a champion for the Gentiles at the council, arguing that they should not place the "yoke" of the law upon the Gentiles (15:10). The reception of the Holy Spirit and the miracle of tongues, witnessed in his preaching to Cornelius's household, had convinced Peter that the distinctive lines between Jews and Gentiles had now been erased (15:9). This testimony served as "the infallible witness to salvation."[200]

Without a doubt, Peter's endorsement would have carried significant weight in favor of the Gentile argument for all those present, including and especially John Mark. After another report was given by Paul and Barnabas on the "signs and wonders" that God had done in their mission to the Gentiles (15:12), another shocking event occurred. This time James, the half brother of Jesus, offered his official statement. A brief mention of James is worth note in order to fully appreciate the weight of his words at the council. James had initially not been a follower (nor a believer) in his half brother as Messiah (John 7:5). Yet, he became a believer when Jesus appeared to him after the resurrection (1 Cor. 15:7). In a short time, James rose to become the undisputed leader of the Jerusalem church and a man

---

[199] Although a consensus is lacking on the exact relationship between these men of "the party of the Pharisees" (Acts 15:5), with the "circumcision group" or the "Judaizers," (Gal. 2:12, Phil. 3:2, Tit. 1:10), they are considered a single group in this text because of their common agenda concerning circumcision of the Gentiles.
[200] Stein, 469.

that even Paul considered a "pillar" within the early church movement (Gal. 2:7). James began with an interesting reference to Peter's testimony: "how God first visited the Gentiles, *to take from them a people for his name"* (15:14). It was evident that God was working to harvest the Gentile world, and the Jews had become the harvest workers. Quoting from Amos 9:11–12, James argued that Amos's prophecy to rebuild David's "booth" was here initiated by God's promised blessing of the Gentiles, and that day had now arrived.[201] James ascribed a theological validation of Paul's claim by demonstrating that, "when the house of David has been re-established, then the Gentiles will come flocking in to share in the blessings that will follow."[202] He now believed that David's house had been restored in the new church initiated by Christ, and the arrival of the Gentiles was, to him, evidence of that restoration. In full agreement of Peter's statement, and full support of Paul's vision, James offered his approval but with certain restrictions.

Although some have argued that the issue at the council concerned primarily "the circumcision of Gentile converts, not the problem of dietary laws,"[203] the biblical evidence demonstrates that both were seriously considered. The debate was not merely theological but in the real and practical way that Jews should associate with Gentile converts at the fellowship table. This is evidenced by James's instructions that the Gentiles continue to abstain from idols, sexual immorality, and foods that have been strangled or contain blood (Acts 15:20). James's mandates appear more closely aligned to the Noachic law than the Mosaic law, and distinctly aimed at the regulations for table fellowship between Jews and Gentiles. Thus, James's decree settled two primary questions raised at the Jerusalem Council. First was the issue of circumcision as a necessity for Gentile salvation, and this was rejected by the Jerusalem leaders. The second question dealt with the more practical issue of Gentiles following

---

[201] J. Paul Tanner, "James' Quotation of Amos 9 to Settle the Jerusalem Council Debate in Acts 15." *Journal of Evangelical Theological Studies* 55, no. 1 (2012): 65–85. https://search-proquest-com.ezproxy.liberty.edu/docview/1018148642?accountid=12085.

[202] N. T. Wright, *Acts for Everyone,* New Testament for Everyone, vol. 2 (Louisville, KY: Westminister John Knox Press, 2008), 44–45.

[203] Jerome Murphy-O'Connor, *Paul: A Critical Life* (Oxford, NY: Oxford University Press, 1997), 132.

minimal dietary restrictions for the sake of Jewish purity laws, and this was approved.[204] James's ruling was accepted by those present, and the new Gentile mission was now officially endorsed by the official Christian church. Interestingly, the traditional method to settle disputes within the rabbinic academies was that "the majority view always prevailed,"[205] and here a compromise was made that clearly favored the church at Antioch. James Dunn[206] appropriately notes that the actions of James and Peter "should be included in the Gentile Christian applause."[207] Most certainly, if not for the leadership and grace extended at the hands of these two pillars of the Jerusalem church, the Gentile mission would have been crippled. For the church at Antioch, the decision of the council was welcome news, since circumcision was viewed as an "abhorrent mutilation of the body"[208] among the Gentiles and a definitive barrier to conversion.

Mark was likely also present at the Jerusalem Council, although neither Luke nor Paul mention him. Mark had returned directly to Jerusalem after leaving Paul and Barnabas at Perga, and the events of the council would certainly have been of the highest importance to him. One can imagine what impact the words of Peter, his mentor, and James, the leader of the Jerusalem church, would have had upon his theology. Mark would have viewed Peter and James as symbols of orthodox Judaism, and their leadership at the council would have likely convicted him to acknowledge his mistake in abandoning Paul and Barnabas at Perga and determine to rejoin his former team when they prepared for their second mission (Acts 15:37). Paul, however, was deeply wounded and refused to recommission Mark for the time being. Despite the success of the Jerusalem Council, the Gentile controversy had inflicted serious damage upon the church.

---

[204] Longenecker, *The Acts of the Apostles*, 448.

[205] Craig S. Keener, *The IVP Bible Background Commentary: New Testament* (Downers Grove, IL: InterVarsity Press, 1993), 365.

[206] James Dunn is Lightfoot Professor Emeritus of Divinity at the University of Durham, England. Few have contributed as greatly to research on the First-Century church and Pauline studies as Dr. Dunn. His three-volume series on *Christianity in the Making* is considered one of the great contributions to NT research today.

[207] Dunn, *Beginning from Jerusalem*, 457.

[208] Gary M. Burge, Lynn H. Cohick, and Gene L. Green, *The New Testament in Antiquity: A Survey of the New Testament Within its Cultural Contexts* (Grand Rapids, MI: Zondervan, 2009), 238.

Relationships needed repair, and a genuine mistrust existed among its leaders (15:38). With the endorsement of the new Gentile mission now in full effect, now was the time to set aside past differences and allow the wounds to mend.

Old Wounds Begin to Mend

A servant of Christ who suffered more than Paul is hard to imagine. Even Jesus anticipated Paul's sufferings when he declared to Ananias, "For I will show him how much he must suffer for the sake of my name" (Acts 9:16). In his surrender to Christ, Paul became a despised object for the Jews, who sought to kill him on numerous occasions (9:23–25, 21:31, 23:12–22), and he was even feared and rejected by the disciples at Jerusalem (9:26). Paul spent a great portion of his Christian life in prison, was stoned nearly to death at Lystra (14:19), suffered from a relentless and incurable "thorn in the flesh," of which the Lord denied healing (2 Cor. 12:7–10), was shipwrecked three times (2 Cor. 11:25), bitten by a venomous snake (Acts 28:3), whipped and beaten on eight different occasions (2 Cor. 11:24–25), repeatedly encountered cold, hunger, and lack of sleep throughout the thousands of miles he journeyed as a missionary, and was eventually martyred as a Christian at Rome. Even on a personal level, Paul sometimes despaired, even of life itself (2 Cor. 1:8), enduring relentless attacks from critics who tried to discredit him (2 Cor. 10:10), churches who weren't loyal to him (2 Cor. 2:4), and false apostles who threatened the stability of his churches (2 Cor. 11:4, Gal. 3:1). Of all his sufferings, it must have been particularly painful for Paul to suffer betrayal at the hands of even his own allies, like John Mark (Acts 13:13), his own disciples (2 Tim. 4:10), and even Barnabas (Gal. 2:13).

Considering the spiritual battles that Paul and Barnabas shared on the mission field, it must have been particularly painful for them when a sharp disagreement over Mark's eligibility to return with them on a second mission caused these two great missionaries to part ways (Acts 15:39). After all, Barnabas had been the means by which Paul had reconnected with the apostles at Jerusalem and had supported Paul at all the major junctions of his ministry. Also likely is that Barnabas's earlier decision to follow Peter's lead in separating from the Gentiles at Antioch (Gal. 2:13) played a role in Paul and Barnabas's "sharp disagreement" over Mark. This is not to say that the damage done by Mark's departure on the first mission did not have a negative impact on Paul and Mark's relationship, for Luke makes it clear that Paul considered Mark unfit precisely because of his withdrawal at Perga in Pamphylia.

From an Ancient Near East perspective, a disciple's abandonment might challenge a teacher's honor.[209] Craig Keener notes, "Even a disciple's abandonment of a teacher's position could be used against the position."[210] Paul experienced a similar betrayal with Demas (2 Tim. 4:10), Jesus with Judas (John 6:64, 71; 13:11), and John with his own flock (1 John 2:19). If the abandonment at Pamphylia were not damaging enough to Mark and Paul's relationship, Mark's report to the Jerusalem church criticizing Paul's work in Pisidia and Lycaonia would have driven the wedge of betrayal even deeper. Worth noting is that John Mark is not heard from again until approximately a decade later, when Paul references Mark as reconciled to his ministry (Col. 4:10, Philem. 24, 2 Tim. 4:11),[211] a clear indication of the consequences of his actions. Of course, one immediate consequence is the parting of ways between Paul and Barnabas. Sadly, these two brothers-in-arms, who had moved mountains together in the way of the Gentile movement, are never mentioned as working together again. However, the good news is that God was not yet done with Mark! The devoted assistant resumed his ministerial work with his cousin Barnabas at Cyprus, and the Spirit of the Lord restored him, not only in his relationship with Paul but also as a symbol of Jewish and Gentile reconciliation for the Christian church.

John Mark: Symbol of Jewish and Gentile Reconciliation?

In many ways, the life and ministry of John Mark, both prior to, and following, the events described in Acts 13:13, have been largely ignored. There is much to derive from Luke's description of the events surrounding

---

[209] Keener, *Acts,* 2031.

[210] Ibid.

[211] James R. Edwards, *The Gospel According to Mark*, The Pillar New Testament Commentary, D. A. Carson, ed. (Grand Rapids, MI: William B. Eerdmans, 2002), 5.

his life and most especially in its meaning for the new Gentile mission that emerged. Mark's life stands as an example of both the division and the reconciliation that occurred within the Gentile controversy, and it seems apparent that Luke fully envisioned for Mark's character to function as such within his narrative. At the onset, he appears to initiate division and controversy. His departure at Perga initiates a tension between himself and Paul that appears to symbolize the initial Jewish rejection of the new Gentile vision. Later, Mark's desire to resume the missionary work with Paul and Barnabas results in a heated disagreement that results in their split (Acts 15:39). As mentioned earlier, Luke would also appear to sketch Mark as a transformative symbol by the way he addressed his name. At first, Luke would intentionally refer to him by his Hebrew identity, either as "John whose other name was Mark" (12:12, 25), or simply as "John" (13:5, 13). Only after the Jerusalem Council does Luke deemphasize the "John" in John Mark's name (15:37) and begin to refer to him exclusively by his Roman name of "Mark" (15:39). Through these literary mechanisms, Luke appears to sketch Mark as a character of division and reconciliation in his plot.

If Luke truly intended to utilize Mark's character as a symbol of the Jewish change toward the Gentile mission, then why did he not explicitly condemn Mark's actions in Acts 13:13? Aside from the various textual clues stressed throughout this investigation, other factors should be considered. To begin with, Luke's apparent silence should not be confused with apathy or ignorance. Luke was reporting on the activities of the early church with an end goal in mind: the eventual victory of the Christian church at the hands of its earliest missionaries. This type of narrative required finesse and masterful character depiction on the part of Luke. Martin Hengel[212] captures this point well:

> So we cannot even claim without further ado, as is the habit of so many scholars today, that Luke only knew what he reported about the early period of Christianity. He certainly knew a good deal more than he put down; when

---

[212] Martin Hengel (1926–2009) served as emeritus professor of NT and Early Judaism for the University of Tübingen, Germany. Dr. Hengel contributed greatly to studies in the Second Temple Period of early Judaism and Christianity.

he is silent about something, there are usually special reasons for it. Only by this strict limitation of his material can he "put his heroes in the right perspective."[213]

Indeed so. Luke did not want to overemphasize the failure surrounding Mark's departure at Perga, because Mark's story does not end there! Luke fully intended to define Mark's life and ministry within the greater narrative of salvation history. Yes, all of Luke's "heroes": Paul, Peter, Barnabas, and even Mark, stumble and fall short of their calling within his chronicle. Yet, they each stand as a microcosm of how God's salvation history works—a perfect God working through imperfect people.

Another point to consider is that Luke and Mark were contemporaries. It would only make sense that Luke does not detail the account of Mark's departure during his first journey because, by the time of the writing of Acts,[214] Mark had already redeemed and restored himself as a credible and reliable missionary. It must be remembered that Luke is writing of his colleagues and is attempting to offer a fair and holistic account of their activities. Luke does not need to expand on the circumstances surrounding Mark's departure at Perga because his readers are already fully aware of the details surrounding this event. This textual feature is known as "intertextuality," which highlights those portions of scripture that contain "presuppositions and associations based upon previous experience."[215] In other words, because Luke knew that the church community was already familiar with Mark's activities during the first Pauline mission, his pausing to detail this episode in Mark's life would not only unfairly ignore the fruitfulness of his post-Jerusalem Council ministry, but also detract from

---

[213] Emphasis added. Martin Hengel, *Acts and the History of Earliest Christianity* (Eugene, OR; Wipf and Stock Publishers, 2003), 36.

[214] Although the dating of Acts varies wildly in current scholarship, Keener's proposal that the dating of Acts (circa AD 70) should be centered around the lifetime of the author, who was likely one of Paul's traveling companions, seems reasonable. For a more thorough discussion on the subject, see Craig S. Keener, *Acts: An Exegetical Commentary,* vol. 1 (Grand Rapids, MI: Baker Academic, 2012), 383–401.

[215] Patricia K. Tull, "Rhetorical Criticism and Intertextuality," *To Each its Own Meaning,* Steven L. McKenzie and Stephen R. Haynes, eds. (Louisville, KY: Westminister John Knox Press, 1999), 165.

his greater objective of establishing Mark as a symbol of Jewish-Gentile reconciliation.

John Mark stands as a symbol of the transformative power of the gospel and the eventual bridge that was formed between Jews and Gentiles. For although Luke clearly described his abandonment of the first mission in a negative fashion, "this need not mean that he would assume that Mark could change … and probably shared the widespread view that character could change over time."[216] Although no indication is made that Paul and Barnabas ever worked together again, we know that Mark eventually regained Paul's trust in ministry. Paul leaves us three textual clues that demonstrate how important Mark became to Paul's ministry after the Jerusalem Council.

1. In his letter to the Colossians, Paul counts Mark as one of only five men "among my fellow workers for the kingdom of God, and they have been a comfort for me" (Col. 4:10–11). If Mark was present with Paul during the writing of Colossians, then it likely places him at Ephesus during the third missionary journey (Acts 19:8–10). This means that Mark rejoined Paul after a brief work with Barnabas at Cyprus and continued his ministry both at Ephesus and possibly Colossae (Col. 4:11). Since Mark had already given spiritual instruction to the Colossians (4:10), Mark likely had already reconnected to the Pauline community even earlier. Interestingly, Paul notes that the Colossians had already "received instructions" from Mark (v. 10), demonstrating that Mark was no longer merely in the background but was actively ministering and teaching God's flock.[217] Nor is the term "instructions" (ἐντολή) insignificant to Paul's description, for he means the type of spiritual

---

[216] Keener, *Acts*, 2031.

[217] Although determining the occasion for Colossians remains unsettled, Mark's apparent freedom to visit the church at Colosse (4:10) suggests that he was either working directly with Paul during this phase of his ministry or working with Peter in Rome and readily available while Paul was imprisoned in Rome. So also the Letter of Philemon, which was likely written under the same circumstances. See Richard R. Melick Jr., *Philippians, Colossians, Philemon*, The New American Commentary, vol. 32 (Nashville, TN: B&H Publishing, 1991).

instructions that can only come from those individuals in a high position within the church.[218]

2. In his letter to Philemon, Paul regards Mark as one of five "fellow workers" (v. 24), working alongside him, most likely at Ephesus.[219] Again, the term "fellow worker" should not be taken lightly, for if Paul wrote Philemon from Ephesus, then this places Mark within the circuit of the churches surrounding Ephesus, working alongside Paul in the mid-fifties.[220] Not only was the term "fellow worker" (συνεργός) endearing to Paul, it was also an honorary title demonstrating his maturity.[221] As mentioned earlier, Mark seemed to have a closer connection to Colossae, where he had already provided biblical instruction, and likely returned to continue the work (Col. 4:10–11). Probably his work at Colossae is where Paul again took notice of Mark and welcomed him back into the fold of his ministry.

3. In what many believe to be his final letter before his martyrdom, Paul specifically requests that Timothy send Mark, because he was "very useful" to his ministry (2 Tim. 4:11). Such a request speaks volumes of Paul's newfound faith in Mark. It is no small matter that Paul now considered Mark as "useful" not merely for personal assistance, as was the case during the first missionary journey (Acts 13:5), but for the teaching ministry (διακονία) of the gospel.[222]

---

[218] BDAG, 3rd ed., 340.

[219] The list of names here is identical to Colossians, except for Jesus Justus, leading many scholars to believe that both letters were written at around the same time and location. Although debatable, a date of AD 52–55, while Paul was working in Ephesus, seems reasonable. See N. T. Wright, *Colossians and Philemon*, Tyndale New Testament Commentaries, vol. 12, Leon Morris, ed. (Grand Rapids, MI: William B. Eerdmans, 1986), 37.

[220] Eduard Lohse, *Colossians and Philemon,* Hermeneia Commentary, Helmut Koester, ed. (Philadelphia: Fortress Press, 1971), 188.

[221] James D. G. Dunn, *Neither Jew Nor Greek: A Contested Identity*, Christianity in the Making, vol. 3. (Grand Rapids, MI: William B. Eerdmans, 2015), 50.

[222] George W. Knight III, *The Pastoral Epistles,* The New International Greek Testament Commentary, I. Howard Marshall and W. Ward Gasque, ed. (Grand Rapids, MI: William B. Eerdmans, 2013), 466.

Mark was no longer the same man who left the shores of Perga and returned to Jerusalem those years ago, and Paul acknowledged it.

As mentioned earlier, Mark would also remain close to his mentor Peter, who would regard Mark as a "son" (1 Pet. 5:13). It is in his colaboring with Peter that Mark is commissioned by the Spirit to produce the work that will forever etch his name in biblical history: the writing of the gospel that bears his name. Eusebius tells the story of how, as Mark ministered alongside Peter in Rome, the people so desperately desired to preserve the words spoken by Peter that they began, "to solicit Mark as the companion of Peter, and whose Gospel we have ... until they prevailed with the man and thus became the means of that history which is called the Gospel according to Mark."[223] We can only imagine what our world would have lost if the church had deemed Mark's initial failure as a forfeiture of his ministry, unable to continue to serve until he was commissioned to write the gospel that offers us Peter's perspective!

Mark remained faithful to the work and ministry of both Jews and Gentiles by his close association to the two primary representatives of each group—Peter and Paul. This would seem to be Luke's intention, to demonstrate Mark's life as a symbol of improved relations between the two worlds. Throughout the story, the Master Potter appears to shape Mark from a reluctant Jew with a narrow vision of God's salvific grace, to the bold missionary that eventually penned a gospel that was written primarily for Gentile nonbelievers.[224] A later tradition has Mark traveling to Egypt, after the deaths of Peter and Paul, where he continued to serve as pastor of the church at Alexandria until his martyrdom in approximately AD 68.[225] Thus, when viewed from a broader perspective, the biblical witness suggests that Mark is much more than just a minor character who abandoned the mission at Perga at Pamphylia. Rather, his life testimony stands as a commanding symbol of the transformative power of Jesus Christ.

---

[223] Eusebius of Caesarea, *Eusebius' Ecclesiastical History*, translated by C. F. Cruse, 2.15 (Peabody, MA: Hendrickson Publishers, 1998), 50.

[224] Mark Dunn, "Mark: The Man and His Gospel," *Biblical Illustrator* 45, no. 3 (Spring, 2019): 71–74.

[225] McBirnie, 195.

CONCLUSION

It has been my aim to deliver an account of Mark's life and ministry in a way that challenges us to rethink the significance of this oft-overlooked individual. There is no person, event, or truth within Scripture that cannot teach us something about the character of God. In my opinion, Mark presents a multifaceted view of both human and divine nature. We find the all-too-common human aspects of reluctance, dogmatism, and fickleness in Mark, but we also see semblances of humility, metamorphosis, and reconciliation that can only derive from our exposure to the Holy Spirit. However, this book is but a primer. Its intention is to initiate a renewed conversation on Mark and his relationship to the Gentile issue in the early church. More research is warranted with the evidence presented in this text, and I look forward to further contributions to this discussion. Although we may never come to full agreement on the life and background behind the first century church, our aim should remain steadfast on reconstructing the context in a way that best responds to the evidence at hand.

Some scholars have suggested that "Mark was not a prominent person in the primitive church [who] had tarnished his reputation by leaving Paul and Barnabas in the middle of a missionary campaign."[226] But is this analysis completely correct? Most certainly implications of leadership were seen and the issue of resolve to do what is right regardless of the cost. This is the call of ministry. Within these parameters, John Mark had clearly failed when he abandoned his initial venture. But did Luke intend for this event to serve as Mark's defining moment? To assume so overlooks the evidence that follows. Shall we say that Peter "tarnished his reputation" for denying

---

[226] James A. Brooks, *Mark*, The New American Commentary, vol. 23, David S. Dockery, ed. (Nashville, TN: B&H Publishing, 1991), 26.

his Lord three times? What does Paul tell us about Mark's supposedly "tarnished reputation" when he later regards him as a "fellow worker for the kingdom of God" (Col. 4:11) and a man who is now "very useful for ministry" (2 Tim. 4:11)? Shall we also declare with certainty that Mark was not a prominent person if he stands as the distinctive figure to serve effectively in both the Petrine and Pauline communities? How many in scripture were so active in both the primitive Jewish and Gentile causes? Should we not be astounded that this seemingly insignificant person, and not one of the prominent disciples of Jesus, was the one elected to write the gospel that now bears his name?

We are left to wonder whether Mark truly understood what was right while standing at the shores of Perga. If his rift with Paul was based on serious theological issues concerning Gentile adherence to the Torah and kosher table fellowship, as this book has argued, then Mark was probably convinced he should not compromise his faith for Paul's new Gentile agenda. As such, Mark's actions, as flawed as they were, indicated conviction to a worldview that many, if not most, traditional Aramaic-speaking Jews also held at that time. Either way, Luke continues his narrative and ensures that Mark is not left behind.

In his analysis of Paul's conversion, Ernst Käsemann[227] discovered:

> It is man's secret nobility to have to reflect about himself in this way, to be compelled to criticize himself, to be forced to confront himself with the question of the right and the true.[228]

Paul encountered his divine revelation on the way to Damascus. Peter experienced his paradigm shift at Joppa. Mark faced his crisis of faith on the shores of Perga at Pamphylia. John Mark is not an anomaly. He is a symbol of what the gospel was intended to accomplish. Within the scope of this analysis, one finds in Mark the hopeful bridge between Jews and Gentiles made possible, not by the Mosaic covenant, but by the new

---

[227] Ernst Käsemann (1906–98) was a German Lutheran theologian and professor of NT in Mainz (1946–51), Göttingen (1951–59) and Tübingen (1959–71).

[228] Ernst Käsemann, *Perspectives on Paul*, translated by Margaret Kohl (Philadelphia: Fortress Press, 1971), 17.

covenant now established through faith in Jesus Christ. What does that tell us about the Christian initiative for Israel today? Should that hope not continue? In the final analysis, the answer to what motivated John Mark to abandon his first missionary journey appears rooted in his narrow vision of God's grace. However, it would seem that he was eventually able to criticize and confront himself with the question of what is right and true and come to distinguish that God had indeed made something new (Isa. 43:19) in order to accomplish the redemptive promise of old (Gen. 12:3).

PROPOSED CHRONOLOGY OF JOHN MARK		
DATE	**EVENT**	**SOURCE**
AD 30–33	Although the identity of the mysterious man in Mark 14:51–52 remains a mystery, Mark possibly may have been present at Jesus's arrest.[229]	Mark 14:51–52
AD 44	John Mark is in a home church belonging to his mother, and likely under Peter's direction.[230]	Acts 12:12
AD 47	John Mark is recruited by Barnabas and Saul to go to Antioch and support their missionary work.[231]	Acts 12:25
AD 47–48	John Mark departs on first missionary expedition to Asia with Paul and Barnabas.[232]	Acts 13:5
AD 48	John Mark leaves the missionary expedition at Perga and returns to Jerusalem.	Acts 13:13
AD 49	Jerusalem Council convenes to address the Gentile question.[233]	Acts 15:2–21
AD 50–52	Mark travels with Barnabas to Cyprus to continue in mission work (coincides with Paul's second mission).[234]	Acts 15:39

---

[229] The theory that Mark inserted an "anonymous signature" in these verses is now more than a century old. See James R. Edwards, *The Gospel According to Mark,* The Pillar New Testament Commentary (Grand Rapids, MI: William B. Eerdmans, 2002), 440. C. E. B. Cranfield also suggests that if this was indeed Mark's intent, it would be "a kind of modest signature to the gospel." See *The Gospel According to St. Mark,* The Cambridge Greek Testament Commentary (Cambridge: Cambridge University Press, 1963), 438.

[230] McBirnie, 193.

[231] McRay, 75.

[232] Ibid.

[233] Thomas D. Lea and David A. Black, *The New Testament: Its Background and Message,* 2nd ed. (Nashville, TN: Broadman & Holman, 2003), 350.

[234] Ibid.

AD 52	Mark leaves Cyprus and travels to Turkey, where he provides spiritual instruction at Colossae.[235]	Col. 4:10
AD 53	Mark reconnects with Paul during his third missionary journey and two-year stay in Ephesus.[236]	Acts 19:8–10. Col. 4:10–11
AD 54	Mark possibly returns to Colossae to continue his service as minister and teacher to the Colossians.	Col. 4:11
AD 62–64	Mark leaves Turkey and heads to Rome ("Babylon") to support Peter's (and later Paul's) ministry.[237]	2 Timothy 4:11, 1 Peter 5:13
AD 65–67	Mark writes his gospel at Peter's request while in Rome.[238]	Eusebius of Caesarea, *Ecclesiastical History*, 2.15.1–2
AD 66–67	Mark leaves Rome for Alexandria after Peter and Paul are martyred by Nero.[239]	Eusebius of Caesarea, *Ecclesiastical History*, 2.16.1

---

[235] N. T. Wright, *Colossians and Philemon,* Tyndale New Testament Commentaries, Leon Morris, ed. (Grand Rapids, MI: William B. Eerdmans, 1986), 37.

[236] Ibid.

[237] Because Peter's epistle notes that Mark is already in Rome, the dating of 1 Peter is a helpful guide to establishing Mark's arrival. Peter H. Davids suggests a probable date of AD 64–68. See *The First Epistle of Peter,* New International Commentary on the New Testament (Grand Rapids, MI: William B. Eerdmans, 1990), 10. See also Lea and Black, who suggest a date of "just before A.D. 64" (532).

[238] C. E. B. Cranfield, *The Gospel According to St. Mark,* The Cambridge Greek Testament Commentary, C. F. D. Moule, ed. (Cambridge: Cambridge University Press, 1963), 8.

[239] Early church traditions associate Peter's death with the Great Fire of Rome under Nero's reign in AD 64, while Paul's martyrdom has been estimated between AD 64–67. See Ivor J. Davidson, *The Birth of the Church,* vol. 1 (Grand Rapids, MI: Baker Books, 2004), 191.

| AD 68 | Mark is martyred while serving as overseer of Alexandria.[240] | Eusebius of Caesarea, *Ecclesiastical History*, 24.1[241] |

---

[240] "Mark" in *The International Standard Bible Ecyclopaedia,* vol. III, James Orr, ed. (Grand Rapids, MI: William B. Eerdmans, 1939), 1987.

[241] Eusebius dates the succession of Mark by Annianus as the eighth year of Nero's reign. Since Roman tradition notes Nero's rule from AD 54–68, this would place the estimated martyrdom of Mark (assuming Annianus's succession was based on Mark's death) in AD 62. This does not seem to coincide with the fact that Mark was clearly with Peter in Rome during the writing of 1 Peter, circa AD 64–68.

BIBLIOGRAPHY

Achtemeier, Paul J., Joel B. Green, and Marianne Meye Thompson. *Introducing the New Testament: Its Literature and Theology*. Grand Rapids, MI: William B. Eerdmans, 2001.

Arichea, Daniel C. Jr., and Eugene A. Nida. *A Translator's Handbook on Paul's Letter to the Galatians*. New York: United Bible Societies, 1976.

Arndt, W., F. W. Danker, W. Bauer and F. W. Gingrich. *A Greek-English Lexicon of the New Testament and Other Early Christian Literature*. 3rd ed. Chicago: University of Chicago Press, 2000.

Barbieri, Louis. *Mark*, Moody Gospel Commentary. Chicago, IL: Moody Press, 1995.

Barclay, William. *The Letters to the Galatians and Ephesians*. The New Daily Study Bible. Louisville, KY: Westminister John Knox Press, 2002.

Barry, J. D., D. Bomar, D. R. Brown, R. Klippenstein, D. Mangum, C. Sinclair Wolcott, W. Widder, eds. *The Lexham Bible Dictionary*. Bellingham, WA: Lexham Press, 2016.

Baur, F. C. *Paul the Apostle of Jesus Christ: His Life and Works, His Epistles and Teachings*. Grand Rapids, MI: Baker Academic, 2011.

Beasley-Murray, G. R. *Baptism in the New Testament*. Grand Rapids, MI: William B. Eerdmans, 1994.

Betz, Hans D. *Galatians*, Hermeneia—A Critical and Historical Commentary on the Bible. Philadelphia: Fortress Press, 1979.

Bock, Darrell L. *Acts*. Baker Exegetical Commentary on the New Testament. Robert W. Yarbrough and Robert H. Stein, eds. Grand Rapids, MI: Baker Academic, 2007.

Booth, Wayne C. *Rhetoric of Fiction*. 2nd ed. Chicago, IL: University of Chicago Press, 1983.

Brooks, James A. *Mark*. The New American Commentary. Vol. 23. Edited by David S. Dockery. Nashville, TN: B&H Publishing, 1991.

Bruce, F. F. *Paul: Apostle of the Heart Set Free*. Grand Rapids, MI: William B. Eerdmans, 1993.

_____. *The Book of the Acts*. The New International Commentary on the New Testament. Revised ed. Edited by Gordon D. Fee. Grand Rapids, MI: William B. Eerdmans, 1988.

_____. *The Epistle to the Galatians*. The New International Greek Testament Commentary. Edited by I. Howard Marshall and W. Ward Gasque. Grand Rapids, MI: William B. Eerdmans, 1982.

Bruner, Frederick Dale. *A Theology of the Holy Spirit: The Pentecostal Experience and the New Testament Witness*. Unicoi, TN: The Trinity Foundation, 2001.

Bultmann, Rudolf. *Primitive Christianity in its Contemporary Setting*. Translated by Reginald H. Fuller. Philadelphia: Fortress Press, 1980.

_____. *Theology of the New Testament*. Translated by Kendrick Grobel. Waco, TX: Baylor University Press, 2007.

Burge, Gary M., Lynn H. Cohick, Gene L. Green. *The New Testament in Antiquity: A Survey of the New Testament within its Cultural Contexts*. Grand Rapids, MI: Zondervan, 2009.

Conzelmann, Hans. *Acts of the Apostles*. Hermeneia. Eldon J. Epp and Christopher R. Matthews, eds. Philadelphia: Fortress Press, 1987.

Couch, Mal, ed. *A Bible Handbook to the Acts of the Apostles*. Grand Rapids, MI: Kregel Publications, 1999.

Cranfield, C. E. B. *The Gospel According to St. Mark*. The Cambridge Greek Testament Commentary. Edited by C. F. D. Moule. Cambridge: Cambridge University Press, 1963.

Davids, Peter H. *The First Epistle of Peter*. New International Commentary on the New Testament. Edited by Gordon D. Fee. Grand Rapids, MI: William B. Eerdmans, 1990.

Davidson, Ivor J. *The Birth of the Church: From Jesus to Constantine*. The Baker History of the Church. Vol. 1. Edited by Tim Dowley. Grand Rapids, MI: Baker Books, 2004.

Deissmann, G. Adolf. *Bible Studies*. Charleston, SC: BiblioBazaar, 2010.

Dibelius, Martin. *Studies in the Acts of the Apostles*. Edited by Heinrich Greeven. Mifflintown, PA: Sigler Press, 1999.

Dunn, James D. G. *Baptism in the Holy Spirit: A Re-examination of the New Testament Teaching on the Gift of the Spirit in Relation to Pentecostalism Today*. Philadelphia: Westminister Press, 1970.

_____. *Beginning from Jerusalem*. Christianity in the Making. Volume 2. Grand Rapids, MI: William B. Eerdmans, 2009.

_____. *Neither Jew nor Greek: A Contested Identity*. Christianity in the Making. Volume 3. Grand Rapids, MI: William B. Eerdmans, 2015.

_____. *The Theology of Paul the Apostle*. Grand Rapids, MI: William B. Eerdmans, 1998.

Dunn, Mark. "Mark: The Man and His Gospel." *Biblical Illustrator*. Vol. 45. no. 3 (Spring, 2019): 71–74.

Edwards, James R. *The Gospel According to Mark*. The Pillar New Testament Commentary. Edited by D. A. Carson. Grand Rapids, MI: William B. Eerdmans, 2002.

Esler, Philip F. *Community and Gospel in Luke-Acts: The Social and Political Motivation of Lucan Theology*. Cambridge: Cambridge University Press, 1987.

_____. "Paul's Contestation of Israel's (Ethnic) Memory of Abraham in Galatians 3." *Biblical Theology Bulletin* 36, no. 1 (Spring 2006): 23–34. http://link.galegroup.com.ezproxy.liberty.edu/apps/doc/A142569511/AONE?u=vic_liberty&sid=AONE&xid=33278689.

Eusebius of Caesarea. *Ecclesiastical History*. Translated by C. F. Cruse. Peabody, MA: Hendrickson Publishers, 2014.

Ferguson, Everett. *Backgrounds of Early Christianity*. 2nd ed. Grand Rapids, MI: William B. Eerdmans, 1993.

Fung, Ronald Y. K. *The Epistle to the Galatians*, The New International Commentary on the New Testament. Edited by Gordon D. Fee. Grand Rapids, MI: William B. Eerdmans, 1988.

Garrett, James Leo, Jr. *Baptist Theology: A Four-Century Study*. Macon, GA: Mercer University Press, 2014.

Garroway, Joshua D. "The Pharisee Heresy: Circumcision for Gentiles in the Acts of the Apostles." *New Testament Studies* 60,

no. 1 (January 2014): 20–36, http://ezproxy.liberty.edu/
login?url=https://search-proquest-com.ezproxy.liberty.edu/
docview/1468235045?accountid=12085.

George, Timothy. *Galatians*. The New American Commentary, vol. 30. Edited by E. Ray Clendenen. Nashville, TN: B&H Publishing, 1994.

Gonzalez, Justo L. *The Story of Christianity: The Early Church to the Dawn of the Reformation*. Vol. 1. Revised edition. New York, NY: Harper One, 2010.

Gonzalez, Rudolph D. *Then Came Hispangelicals: The Rise of the Hispanic Evangelical and Why It Matters*. Sisters, OR: Deep River Books, 2019.

Guthrie, Donald. *New Testament Introduction*. Downers Grove, IL: InterVarsity Press, 1970.

Guy, Laurie. *Introducing Early Christianity: A Topical Survey of Its Life, Beliefs, & Practices*. Downers Grove, IL: InterVarsity Press, 2004.

Hawthorne, Gerald F., Ralph P. Martin, eds. *Dictionary of Paul and His Letters*. Downers Grove, IL: InterVarsity Press, 1993.

Hengel, Martin. *Acts and the History of Earliest Christianity*. Translated by John Bowden. Eugene, OR: Wipf and Stock Publishers, 2003.

Hoehner, Harold W. *Ephesians: An Exegetical Commentary*. Grand Rapids, MI: Baker Academic, 2004.

Hoogendyk, Isaiah, David DeSilva, Randall Tan, and Rick Brannan, eds. *The Lexham Analytical Lexicon to the Septuagint*. Bellingham, WA: Lexham Press, 2012.

Instone-Brewer, David. "The Eighteen Benedictions and the Minim Before 70 CE." *Journal of Theological Studies* 54, no. 1. (April 2003): 25–44. https://doi-org.ezproxy.liberty.edu/10.1093/jts/54.1.25.

Johnson, Luke Timothy. *Among the Gentiles: Greco-Roman Religion and Christianity*. The Anchor Yale Bible Reference Library. New Haven, CT: Yale University Press, 2009.

Josephus, Flavius. *Josephus: The Complete Works*. Translated by William Whiston. Nashville, TN: Thomas Nelson, 1998.

Käsemann, Ernst. *Perspectives on Paul*. Translated by Margaret Kohl. Philadelphia: Fortress Press, 1971.

Keener, Craig S. *Acts: An Exegetical Commentary*. Vol. 2. Grand Rapids, MI: Baker Academic, 2013.

_____. *Galatians: A Commentary*. Grand Rapids, MI: Baker Academic, 2019.

_____. *The IVP Bible Background Commentary: New Testament*. Downers Grove, IL: InterVarsity Press, 1993.

Kent, Homer A., Jr. *Jerusalem to Rome: Studies in the Book of Acts*. Winona Lake, IN: BMH Publishing, 1985.

Kim, Seyoon. *The Origin of Paul's Gospel*. Eugene, OR: Wipf & Stock Publishers, 2007.

Kittel, G. and G. W. Bromiley, Eds. *Theological Dictionary of the New Testament*. Volume 8. Grand Rapids, MI: Eerdmans, 2006.

Knight, George W. III. *The Pastoral Epistles*. The New International Greek Testament Commentary. Edited by I. Howard Marshall and W. Ward Gasque. Grand Rapids, MI: William B. Eerdmans, 2013.

Knowling, R. J. *The Acts of the Apostles*. The Expositor's Greek Testament. Edited by W. Robertson Nicoll. Vol II. Grand Rapids, MI: William B. Eerdmans, 1983.

Köstenberger, Andreas J. *Encountering John: The Gospel in Historical, Literary, and Theological Perspective*. 2nd ed. Grand Rapids, MI: Baker Academic, 2013.

Kuhn, Karl G. *Theological Dictionary of the New Testament*. Vol. VI. Edited by Gerhard Friedrich. Translated & Edited by Geoffrey W. Bromiley. Grand Rapids, MI: William B. Eerdmans, 1968.

Langer, Ruth. *Cursing the Christians? A History of the Birkat Haminim*. New York, NY: Oxford University Press, 2012.

Lea, Thomas D. and David A. Black. *The New Testament: Its Background and Message*. 2nd ed. Nashville, TN: Broadman & Holman Publishers, 2003.

Liddell, H. G., Scott, R., Jones, H. S., & McKenzie, R. *A Greek-English Lexicon*. Oxford, NY: Clarendon Press, 1996.

Lohse, Eduard. *Colossians and Philemon*. Hermeneia Commentary. Edited by Helmut Koester. Philadelphia: Fortress Press, 1971.

Longenecker, Richard N. *Galatians*. Word Biblical Commentary. Vol. 41. Edited by Ralph P. Martin. Dallas, TX: Word Books, 1990.

_____. *The Acts of the Apostles*. The Expositor's Bible Commentary. Vol. 9. Edited by Frank E. Gaebelein. Grand Rapids, MI: Zondervan, 1981.

Machen, J. Gresham. *The Origin of Paul's Religion*. Middletown, DE: Pantianos Classics, 2017.

Marcus, Joel. "*Birkat Ha-Minim* Revisited." *Journal of New Testament Studies* 55, no. 4 (Oct. 2009): 523–51. doi:http://dx.doi.org. ezproxy.liberty.edu/10.1017/S0028688509990063.

Marshall, I. Howard. *Acts*. Tyndale New Testament Commentaries. vol. 5. Edited by Leon Morris. Downers Grove, IL: Inter-Varsity Press, 2008.

Martyn, J. Louis. *History and Theology in the Fourth Gospel*. 3rd ed. Louisville, KY: Westminister John Knox Press, 2003.

McBirnie, William S. *The Search for the Twelve Apostles*. Revised ed. Carol Stream, IL: Tyndale House Publishers, 2004.

McKenzie, Steven L. and Stephen R. Haynes, eds. *To Each its Own Meaning*, Louisville, KY: Westminister John Knox Press, 1999.

McKnight, Scot. *Galatians*. The NIV Application Commentary. Edited by Terry Muck. Grand Rapids, MI: Zondervan, 1995.

McRay, John. *Paul: His Life and Teaching*. Grand Rapids, MI: Baker Academic, 2004.

Melick, Richard R. Jr. *Philippians, Colossians, Philemon*. The New American Commentary. Vol. 32. Nashville, TN: B&H Publishing, 1991.

Metzger, Bruce M. *A Textual Commentary on the Greek New Testament*. 2nd ed. Deutsche Bibelgesellschaft, 2016.

Meyer, Jason C. *The End of the Law: Mosaic Covenant in Pauline Theology*. NAC Studies in Bible & Theology. Edited by E. Ray Clendenen. Nashville, TN: B&H Publishing Group, 2009.

Moo, Douglas J. *Galatians*. Baker Exegetical Commentary on the New Testament. Edited by Robert W. Yarbrough and Robert H. Stein. Grand Rapids, MI: Baker Academic, 2013.

Morgan, G. Campbell. *The Acts of the Apostles*. New York, NY: Fleming H. Revell, 1924.

Morris, Leon. *Galatians: Paul's Charter of Christian Freedom*. Downers Grove, IL: InterVarsity Press, 1996.

Murphy-O'Connor, Jerome. *Paul: A Critical Life*. New York, NY: Oxford University Press, 1997.

Nanos, Mark D., Magnus Zetterholm, eds. *Paul Within Judaism: Restoring the First-Century Context to the Apostle*. Minneapolis, MN: Fortress Press, 2015.

Nicklas, Tobias and Herbert Schlögel. "Mission to the Gentiles: The Construction of Christian Identity and its Relationship with Ethics According to Paul." *Hervormde Teologiese Studies* 68, no. 1 (2012): 1–7, http://ezproxy.liberty.edu/login?url=https://search-proquest-com.ezproxy.liberty.edu/docview/1283226276?accountid=12085.

Niederwimmer, K. & H. W. Attridge. *The Didache: A Commentary*. Hermeneia Series. Minneapolis, MN: Fortress Press, 1998.

Orr, James, ed. *The International Standard Bible Encyclopaedia*. Grand Rapids, MI: William B. Eerdmans, 1939.

Perrin, Norman and Dennis C. Duling. *The New Testament: An Introduction*. 2nd ed. San Diego, CA: Harcourt Brace Jovanovich, 1982.

Polhill, John B. *Paul and His Letters*. Nashville, TN: B&H Academic, 1999.

Pollock, John. *The Apostle: A Life of Paul*. Colorado Springs, CO: ChariotVictor Publishing, 1985.

Powell, Mark Allan. *What is Narrative Criticism?* Minneapolis, MN: Fortress Press, 1990.

Ramsay, William M. *St. Paul: The Traveler and Roman Citizen*. Revised ed. Edited by Mark Wilson. Grand Rapids, MI: Kregel Publications, 2001.

Ridderbos, Herman. *Paul: An Outline of His Theology*. Translated by John R. De Witt. Grand Rapids, MI: William B. Eerdmans, 1997.

Robertson, A. T. *The Acts of the Apostles*. Word Pictures in the New Testament. Vol. III Nashville, TN: Broadman Press, 1930.

Ryken, Philip G. *Galatians*. Reformed Expository Commentary. Edited by Daniel M. Doriani. Phillipsburg, NJ: P&R Publishing, 2005.

Sampley, J. Paul, ed. *Paul in the Greco-Roman World*. Harrisburg, PA: Trinity Press International, 2003.

Sanders, E. P. *Paul and Palestinian Judaism*. Philadelphia: Fortress Press, 1977.

Segal, Alan F. *Paul the Convert: The Apostolate and Apostasy of Saul the Pharisee*. New Haven, CT: Yale University Press, 1990.

Schaser, N. J. "Unlawful for a Jew? Acts 10:28 and the Lukan View of Jewish-Gentile Relations." *Biblical Theology Bulletin* 48, no. 4 (2018): 188–201, https://doi.org/10.1177/0146107918801512.

Schliesser, Benjamin. "'Christ-Faith' as an Eschatological Event (Galatians 3:23–26): A 'Third View' on Πίστις Χριστοῦ," *Journal for the Study of the New Testament* 38, no. 3 (2016): 283. sagepub.co.uk/journalsPermissions.nav.

Schreiner, Thomas R. *Galatians*. Zondervan Exegetical Commentary on the New Testament. Edited by Clinton E. Arnold. Grand Rapids, MI: 2010.

_____. *New Testament Theology: Magnifying God in Christ* (Grand Rapids, MI: Baker Academic, 2008), 444

_____. *Paul, Apostle of God's Glory in Christ: A Pauline Theology*. Downers Grove, IL: InterVarsity Press, 2001.

Scott, J. Julius, Jr. *"The Cornelius Incident in the Light of its Jewish Setting,"* *Journal of Evangelical Theological Society* 34, no. 4 (December 1991), 475–84.

Sheldon, Henry C. *History of the Christian Church: The Early Church*. Vol. 1. Peabody, MA: Hendrickson Publishers, 1988.

Silva, Moises. "Galatians," *Commentary on the New Testament Use of the Old Testament*. Edited by G. K. Beale and D. A. Carson. Grand Rapids, MI: Baker Academic, 2007. http://ebookcentral.proquest.com/lib/liberty/detail.action?docID=3117030.

Slee, Michelle. *The Church in Antioch in the First Century C.E.: Communion and Conflict*. The Sheffield Journal for the Study of the New Testament Supplement Series. Edited by Stanley E. Porter. New York: T & T Clark International, 2003.

Stendahl, Krister. *Paul among Jews and Gentiles*. Philadelphia: Fortress Press, 1978.

Stott, John R. W. *The Message of Acts: The Spirit, the Church and the World*. The Bible Speaks Today. Edited by John R. W. Stott. Downers Grove: IL: Inter-Varsity Press, 1990.

Sumney, Jerry L. *Paul: Apostle and Fellow Traveler*. Nashville, TN: Abingdon Press, 2014.

Tanner, J. Paul. "James' Quotation of Amos 9 to Settle the Jerusalem Council Debate in Acts 15." *Journal of Evangelical Theological Studies* 55, no. 1 (2012): 65–85. https://search-proquest-com.ezproxy.liberty.edu/docview/1018148642?accountid=12085.

Tenney, Merrill C. *New Testament Times: Understanding the World of the First Century.* Grand Rapids, MI: Baker Books, 2002.

The International Standard Bible Encyclopaedia, vol. III, James Orr, ed. Grand Rapids, MI: William B. Eerdmans, 1939.

Thornhill, A. Chadwick. *The Chosen People: Election, Paul and Second Temple Judaism.* Downers Grove, IL: InterVarsity Press, 2015.

Vanhoozer, Kevin J., ed. *Theological Interpretation of the New Testament.* Grand Rapids, MI: Baker Academic, 2009.

Waltke, Bruce K. *Genesis: A Commentary.* Grand Rapids, MI: Zondervan, 2001.

Wallace, Daniel B. *Greek Grammar: Beyond the Basics.* Grand Rapids, MI: Zondervan, 1996.

Wellhausen, Julius. *Prolegomena to the History of Ancient Israel.* Cambridge: Cambridge University Press, 2013.

Wenham, David. *Paul: Follower of Jesus or Founder of Christianity?* Grand Rapids, MI: William B. Eerdmans, 1995.

Wiarda, Timothy. "The Jerusalem Council and the Theological Task." *Journal of the Evangelical Theological Society* 46, no. 2 (June 2003): 233, http://ezproxy.liberty.edu/login?url=https://search-proquest-com.ezproxy.liberty.edu/docview/211144651?accountid=12085.

Witherington, Ben III. *New Testament History: A Narrative Account.* Grand Rapids, MI: Baker Academic, 2001.

_____. *Paul's Narrative Thought World: The Tapestry of Tragedy and Triumph.* Louisville, KY: Westminister/John Knox Press, 1994.

_____. *The Acts of the Apostles: A Socio-Rhetorical Commentary.* Grand Rapids, MI: William B. Eerdmans, 1998.

Wright, N. T. *Acts for Everyone.* New Testament for Everyone. Vol. 2. Louisville, KY: Westminister John Knox Press, 2008.

_____. *Colossians and Philemon.* Tyndale New Testament Commentaries. Vol. 12. Edited by Leon Morris. Grand Rapids, MI: William B. Eerdmans, 1986.

_____. *Paul: A Biography.* New York, NY: HarperCollins, 2018.

CPSIA information can be obtained
at www.ICGtesting.com
Printed in the USA
BVHW031331160720
583884BV00005B/44/J

9 781973 695073